THE WORLD'S M
BEAUTIFUL MUSIC

Ballads · Standards
Show Tunes · Movie Themes

MW00443327

CONTENTS

Produced by
Alfred Music
P.O. Box 10003
Van Nuys, CA 91410-0003
alfred.com

ISBN-10: 0-7390-6834-2
ISBN-13: 978-0-7390-6834-2

Cover photo: © Veer Incorporated

ANGEL EYES

Composed by Jim Brickman
Arranged by Dan Coates

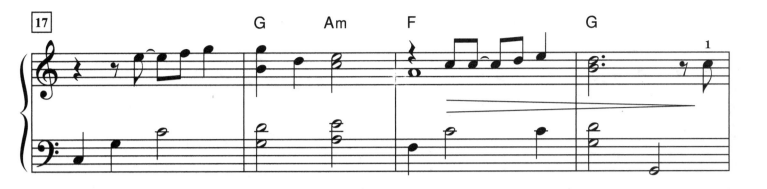

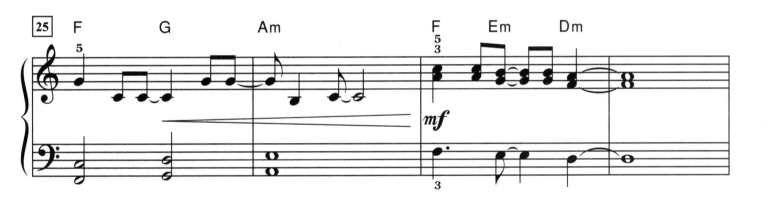

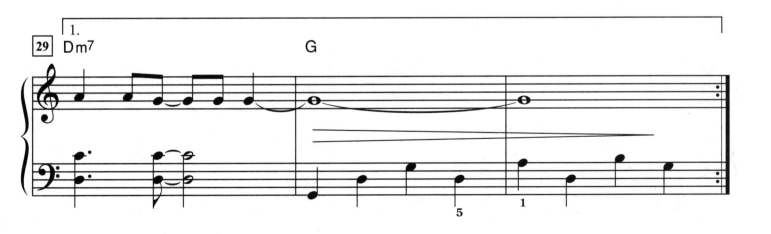

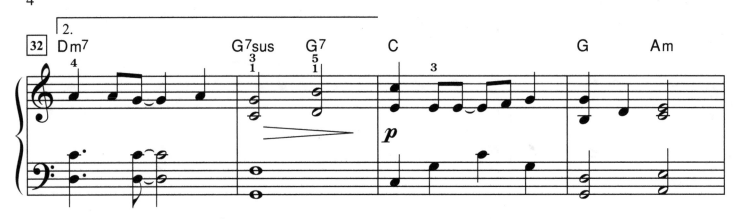

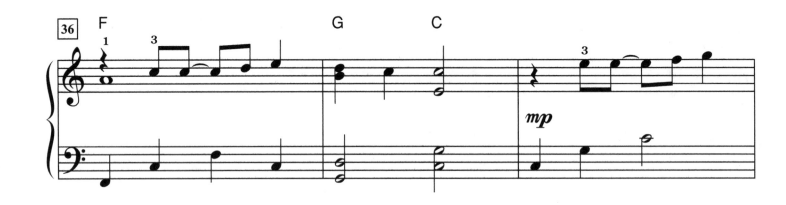

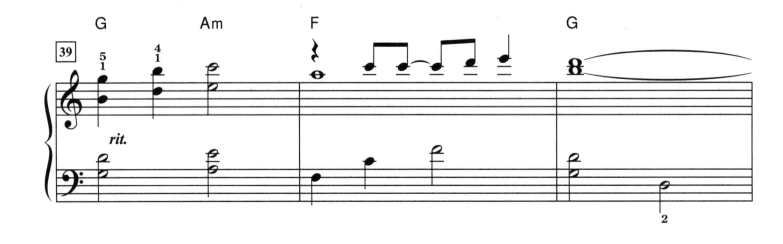

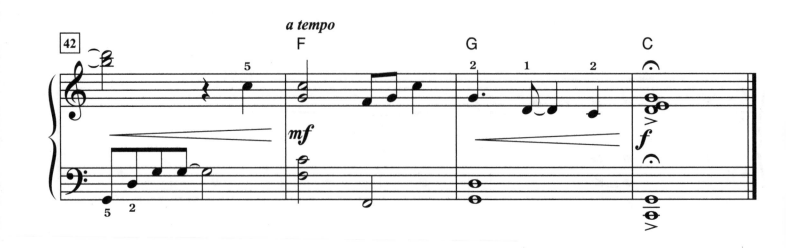

AS TIME GOES BY

(from "Casablanca")

Words and Music by Herman Hupfeld
Arranged by Dan Coates

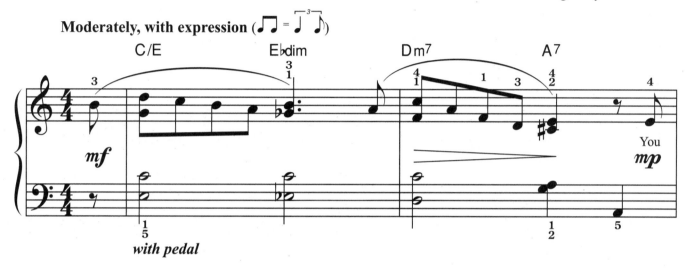

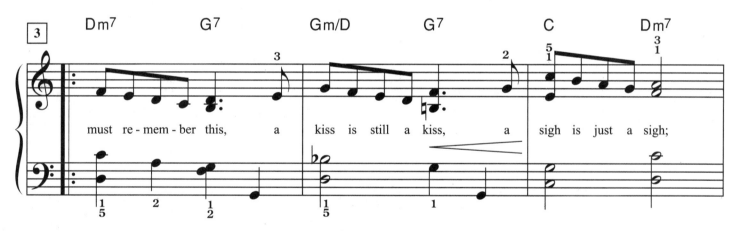

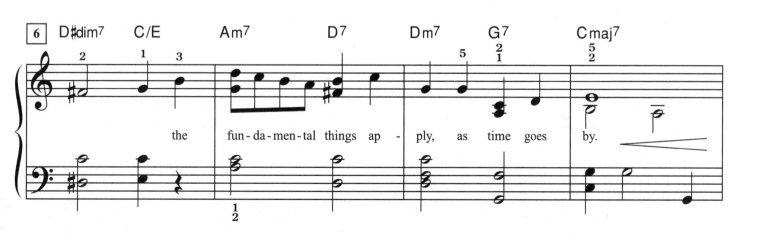

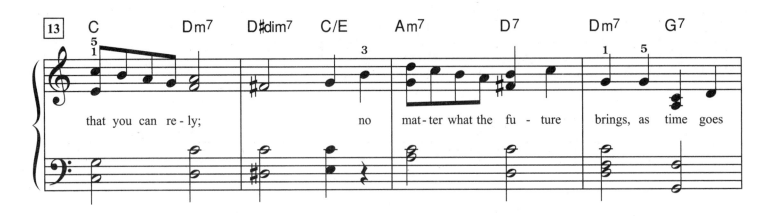

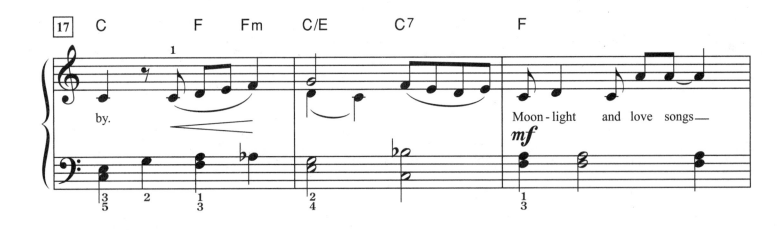

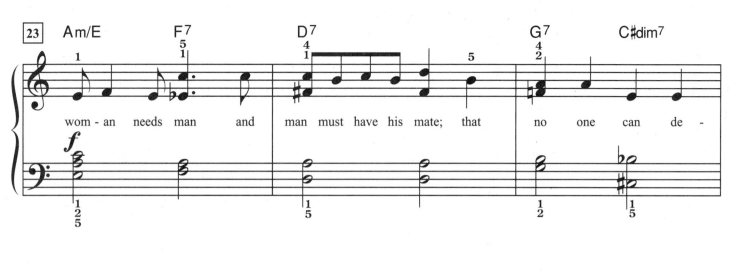

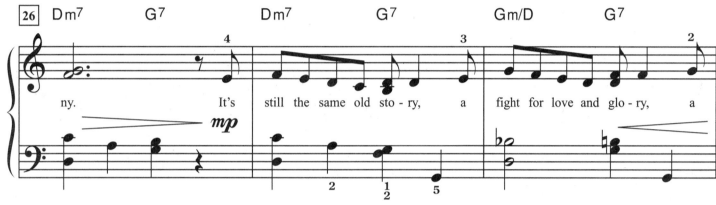

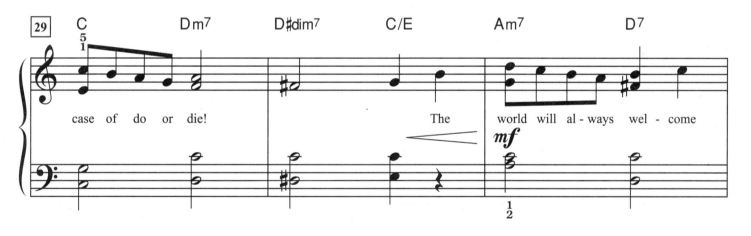

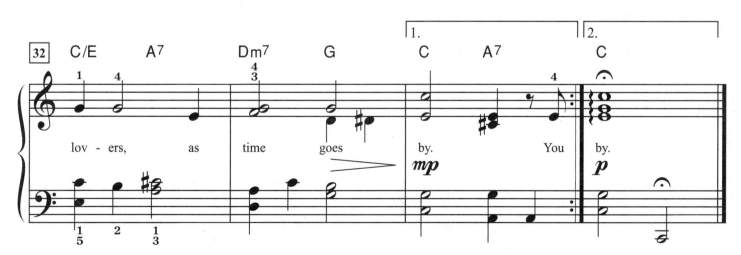

AT LAST

Music by Harry Warren
Lyrics by Mack Gordon
Arranged by Dan Coates

BECAUSE YOU LOVED ME

(Theme from "Up Close and Personal")

Words and Music by Diane Warren
Arranged by Dan Coates

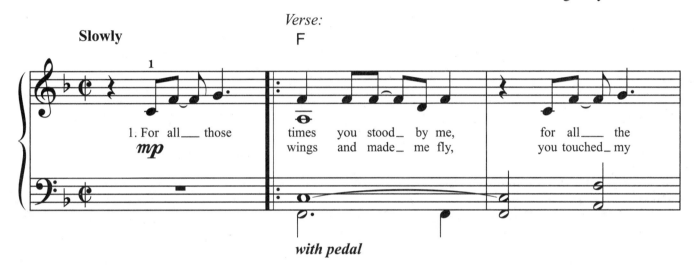

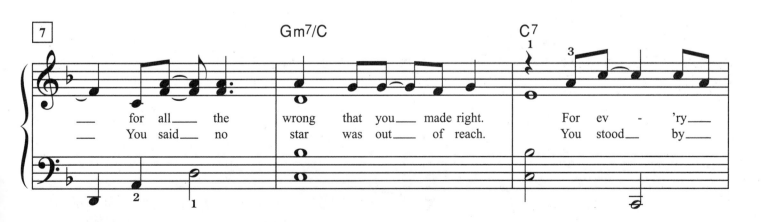

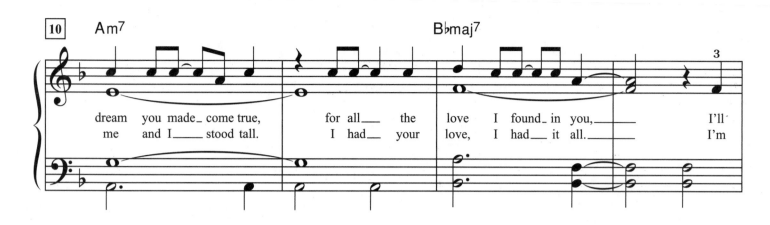

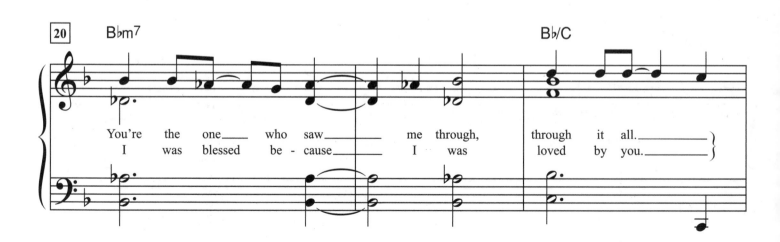

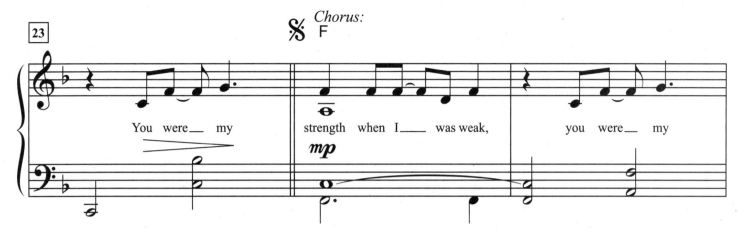

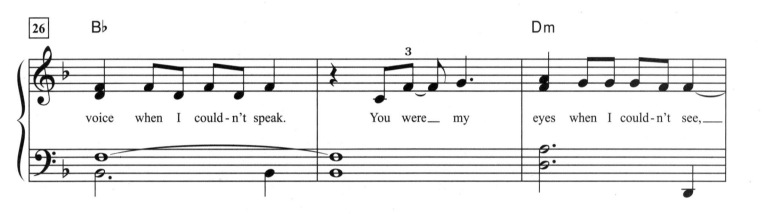

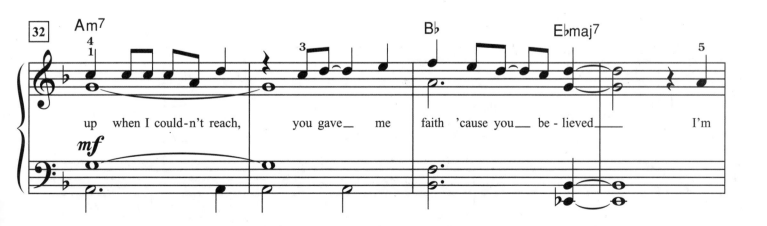

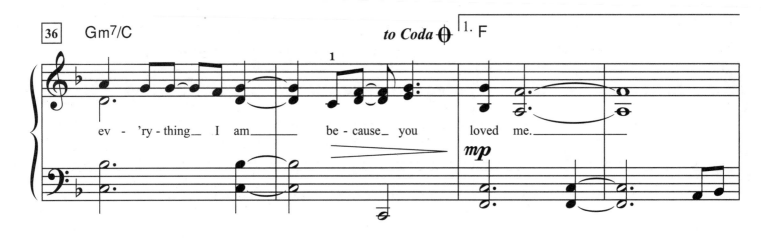

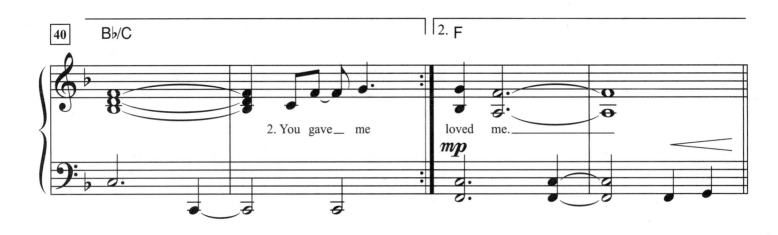

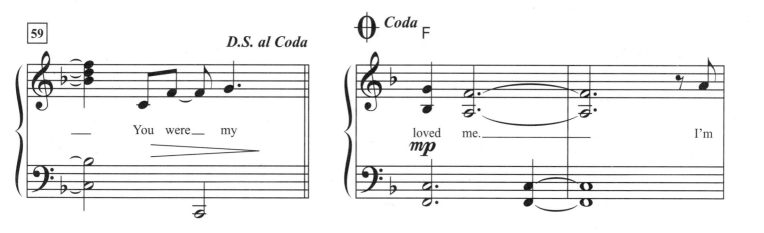

BEWITCHED, BOTHERED, AND BEWILDERED

(from "Pal Joey")

Words by Lorenz Hart
Music by Richard Rodgers
Arranged by Dan Coates

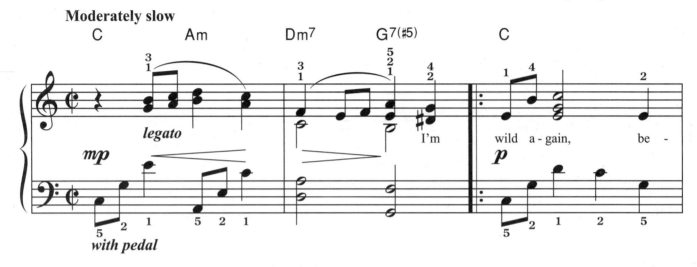

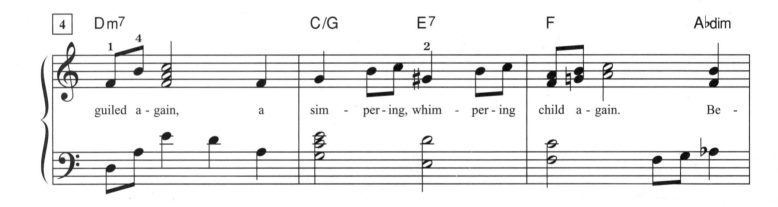

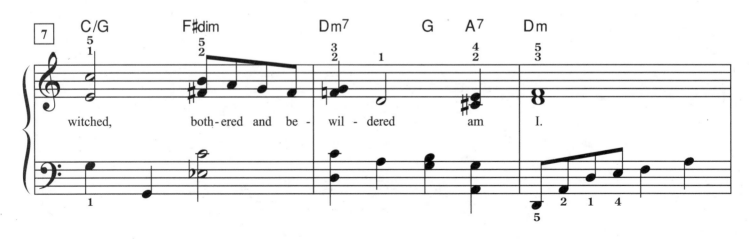

Could-n't sleep,   and   would-n't sleep   when

love came and told me I should-n't sleep.   Be - witched,   both-ered and be-

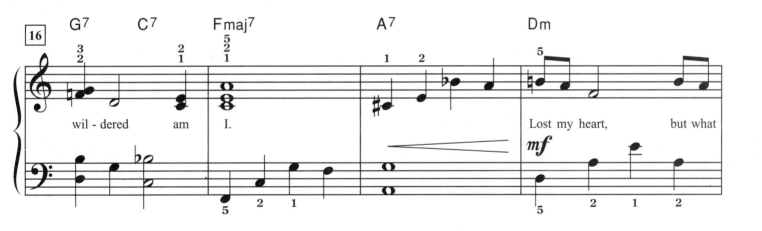

wil - dered   am   I.   Lost my heart,   but what

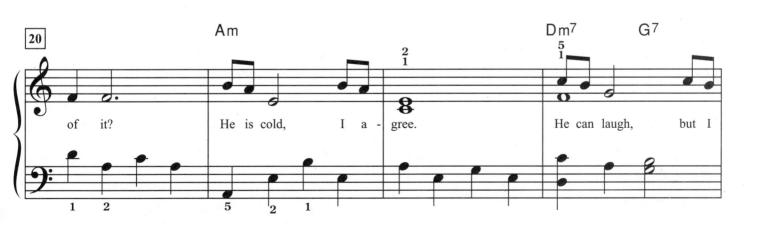

of it?   He is cold,   I a - gree.   He can laugh,   but I

love it, al - though the laugh's on me. I'll

sing to him, each spring to him, and long for the day when I'll

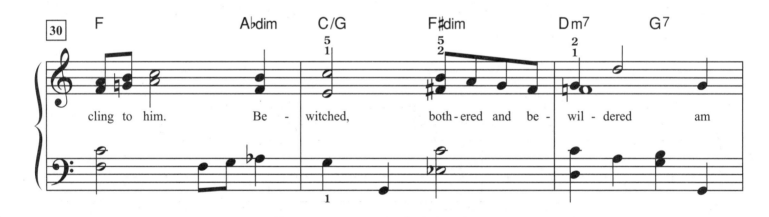

cling to him. Be - witched, both-ered and be - wil - dered am

I'm

I.

COME RAIN OR COME SHINE

Lyrics by Johnny Mercer
Music by Harold Arlen
Arranged by Dan Coates

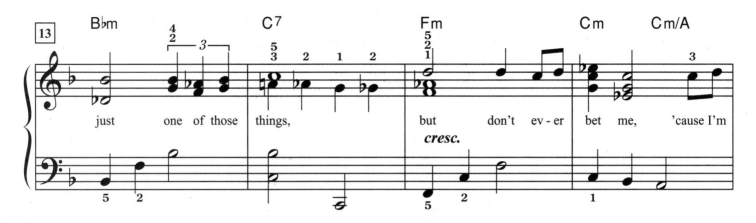

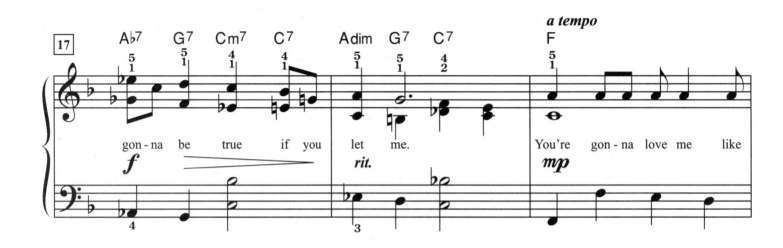

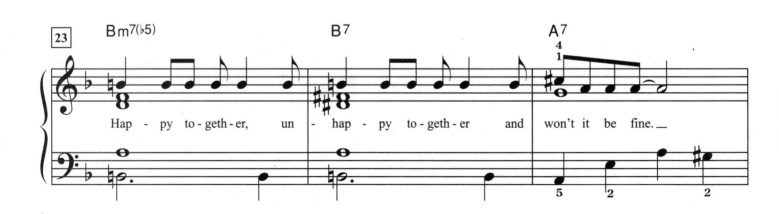

BRIDGE OVER TROUBLED WATER

Words and Music by Paul Simon
Arranged by Dan Coates

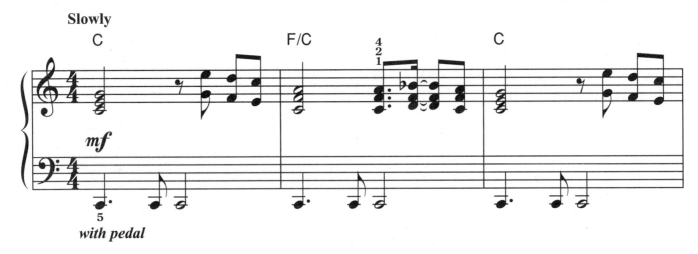

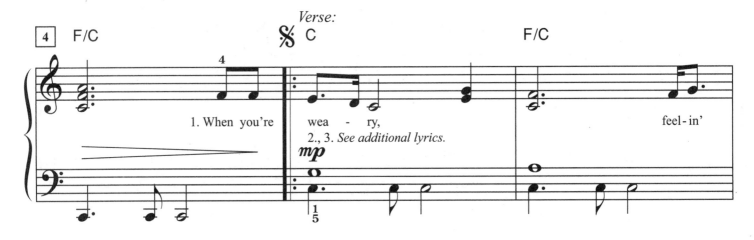

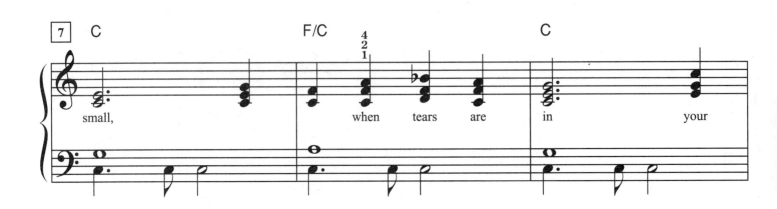

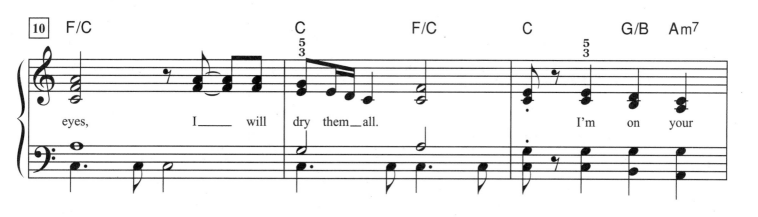

Chorus:

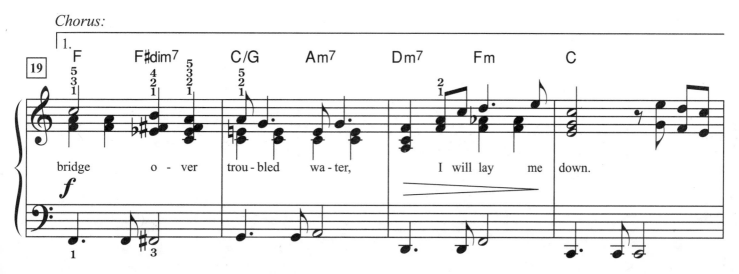

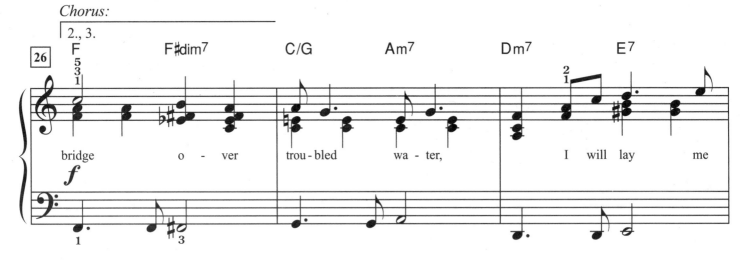

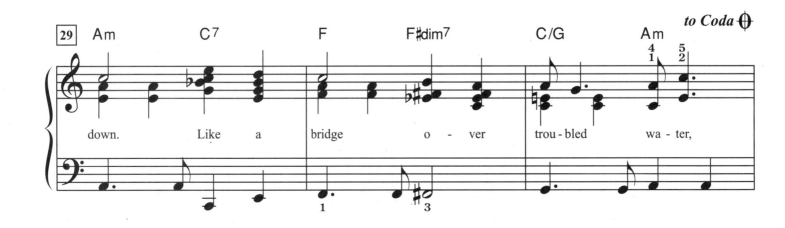

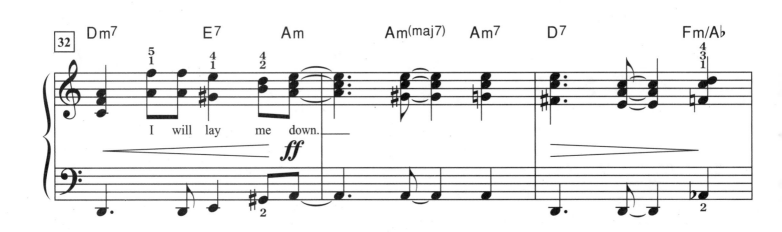

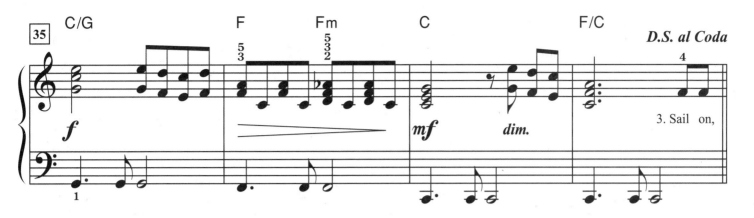

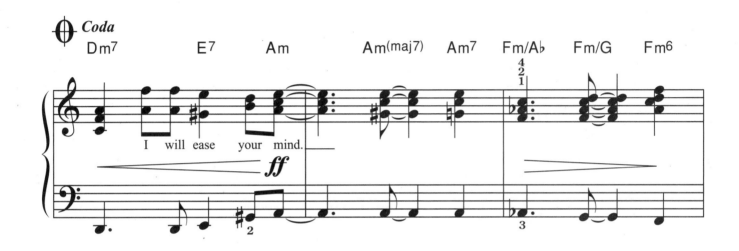

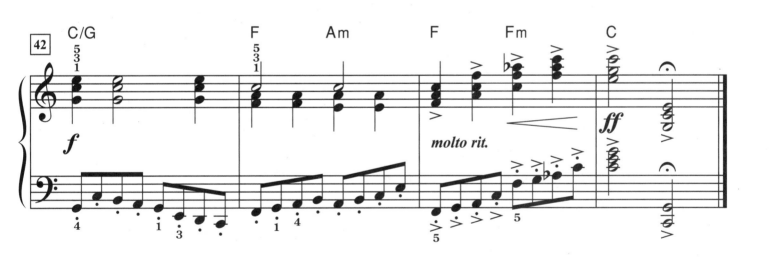

Verse 2:
When you're down and out,
When you're on the street,
When evening falls so hard, I will comfort you.
I'll take your part when darkness comes
And pain is all around.
Like a bridge over troubled water, I will lay me down.
Like a bridge over troubled water, I will lay me down.

Verse 3:
Sail on, silver girl, sail on by.
Your time has come to shine,
All your dreams are on their way.
See how they shine, if you need a friend.
I'm sailing right behind.
Like a bridge over troubled water, I will ease your mind.
Like a bridge over troubled water, I will ease your mind.

CANON IN D

By Johann Pachelbel
Arranged by Dan Coates

THE DAYS OF WINE AND ROSES

Lyric by Johnny Mercer
Music by Henry Mancini
Arranged by Dan Coates

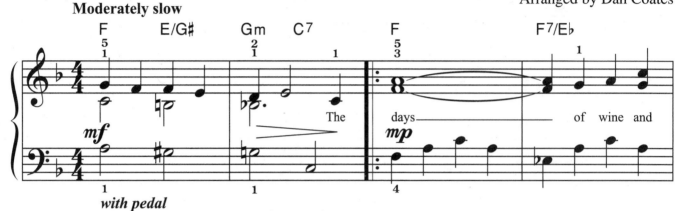

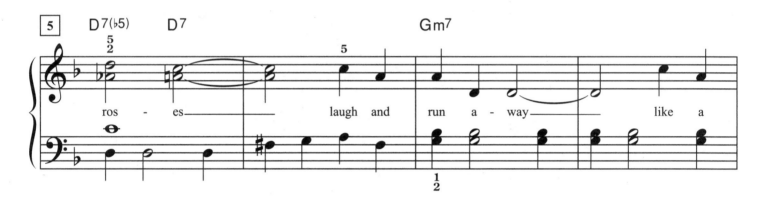

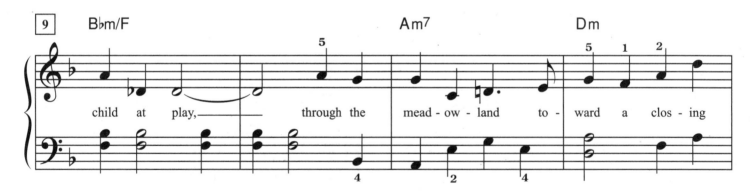

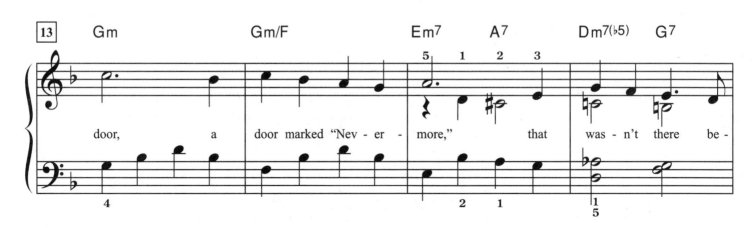

ENDLESS LOVE

Words and Music by Lionel Richie
Arranged by Dan Coates

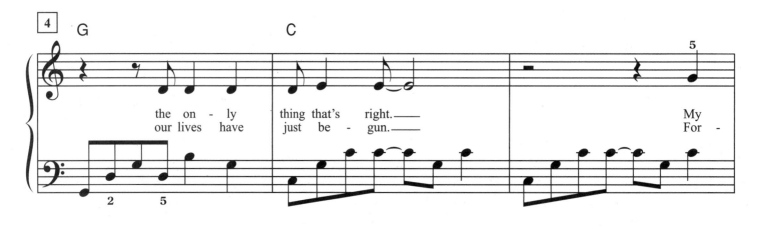

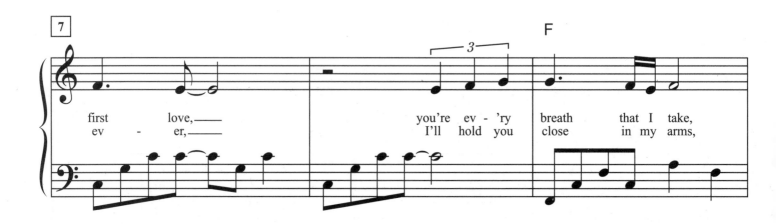

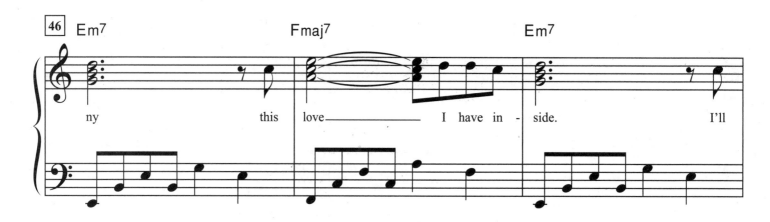

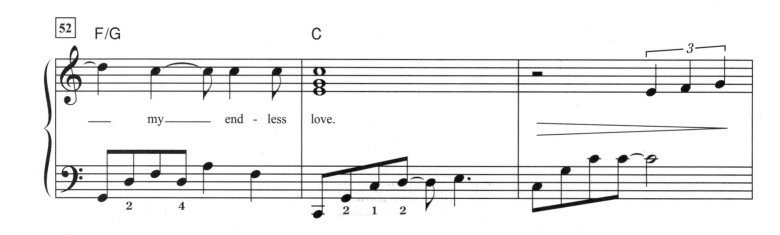

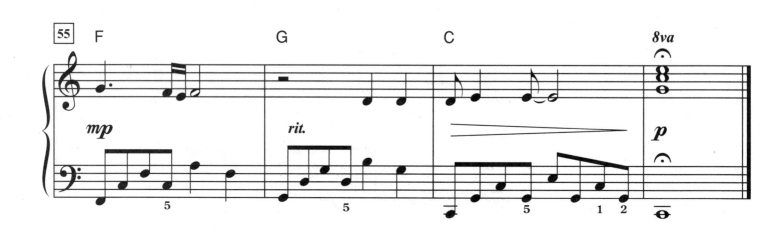

FALLING SLOWLY

(from "Once")

Words and Music by
Glen Hansard and Marketa Irglova
Arranged by Dan Coates

Slowly, with expression

Verse:

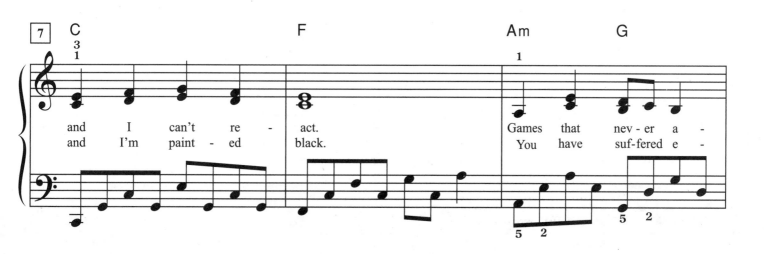

HERO

Words and Music by
Walter Afanasieff and Mariah Carey
Arranged by Dan Coates

HOME

Words and Music by
Michael Bublé, Alan Chang And Amy Foster
Arranged by Dan Coates

Moderately slow

Lyrics (line 1): An- oth- er sum- mer day has come and gone a- way

Lyrics (line 2): in Par- is and Rome, — but I wan- na go home. —

Lyrics (line 3): May be sur- round- ed by a mil- lion peo- ple; I still feel all a- lone, —

HOW COULD I EVER KNOW?

(from "The Secret Garden")

Lyrics by Marsha Norman
Music by Lucy Simon
Arranged by Dan Coates

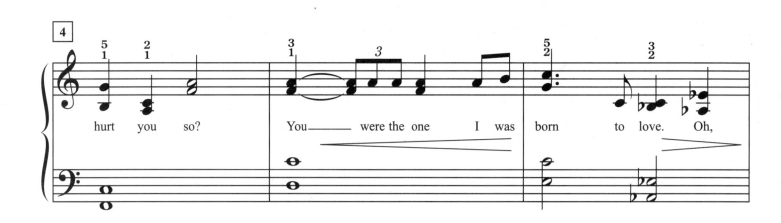

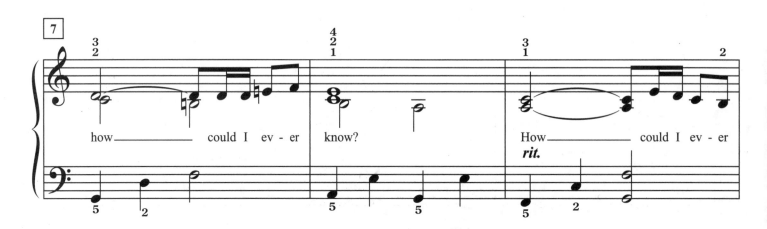

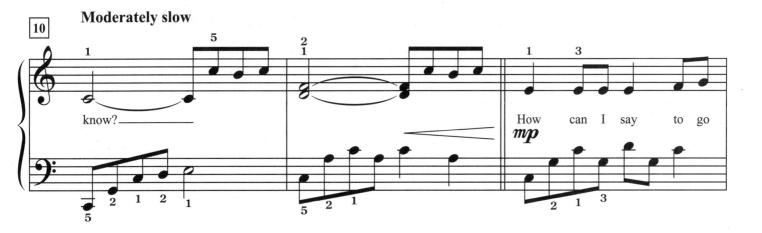

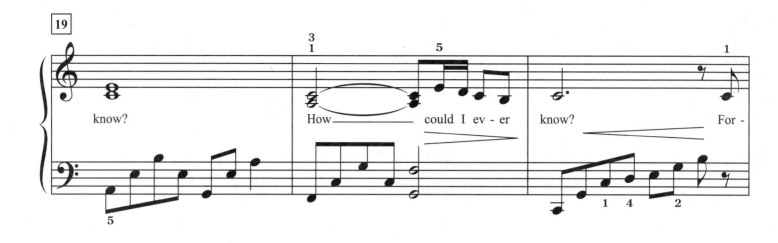

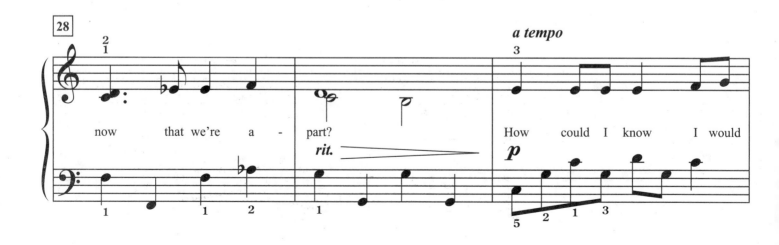

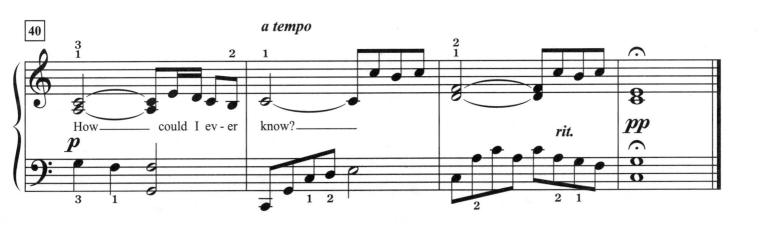

HOW DEEP IS YOUR LOVE

Words and Music by
Barry Gibb, Maurice Gibb And Robin Gibb
Arranged by Dan Coates

Moderately, with a steady beat

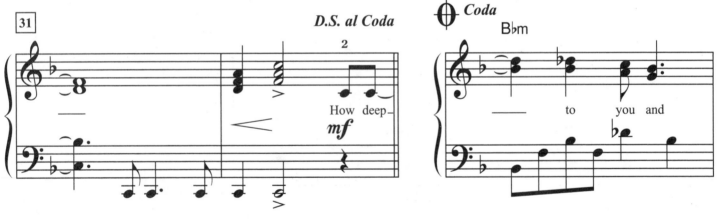

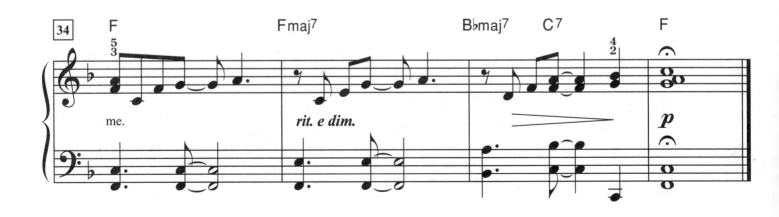

HOW DO I LIVE

Words and Music by Diane Warren
Arranged by Dan Coates

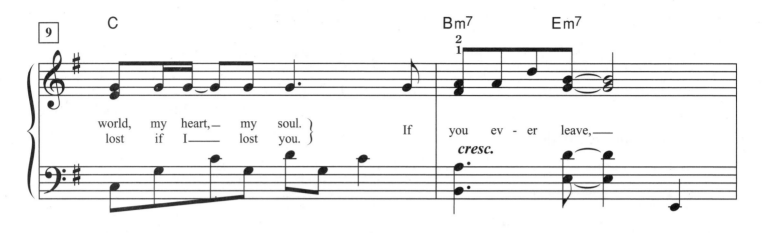

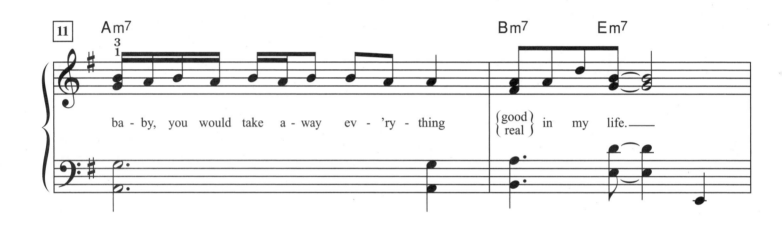

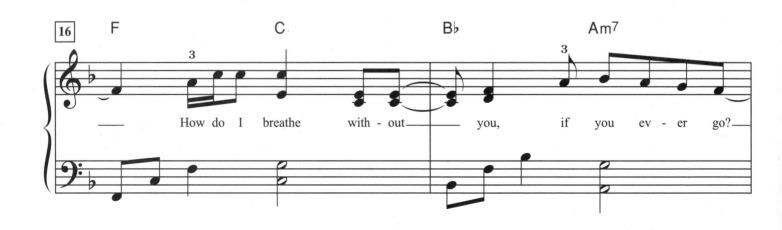

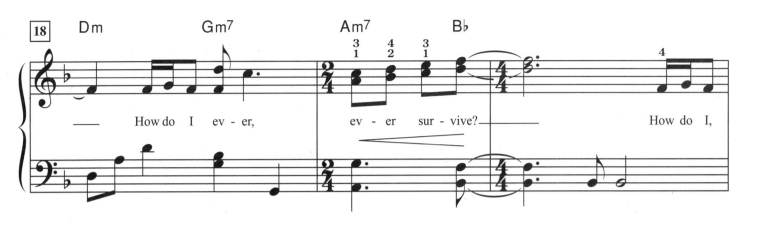

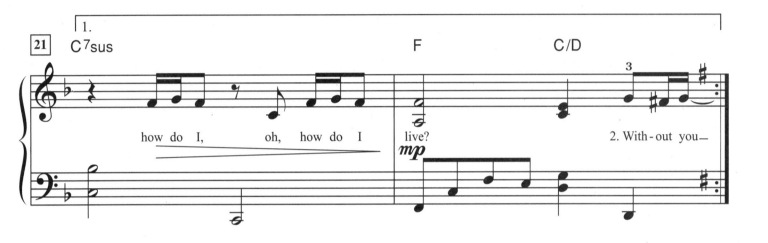

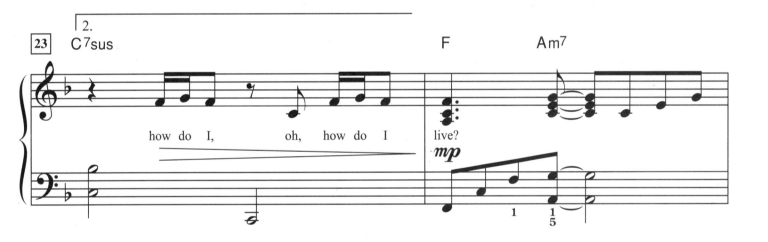

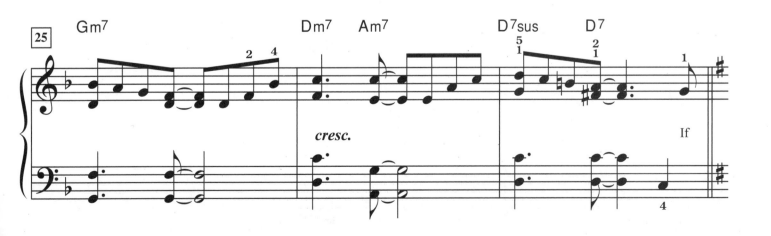

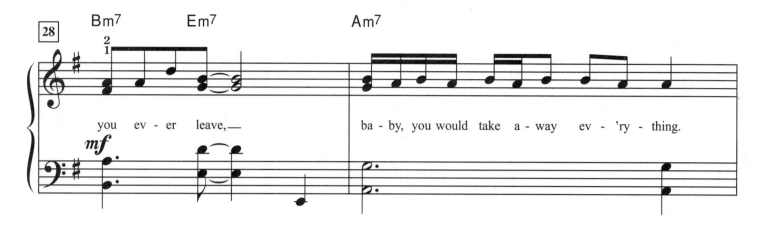

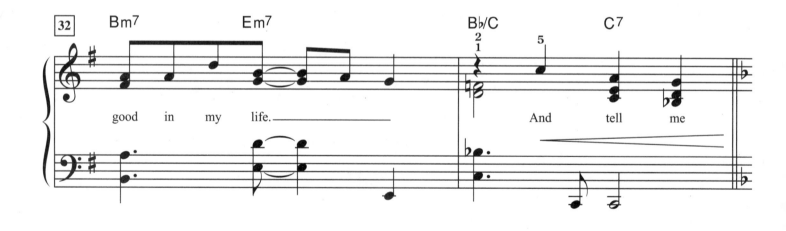

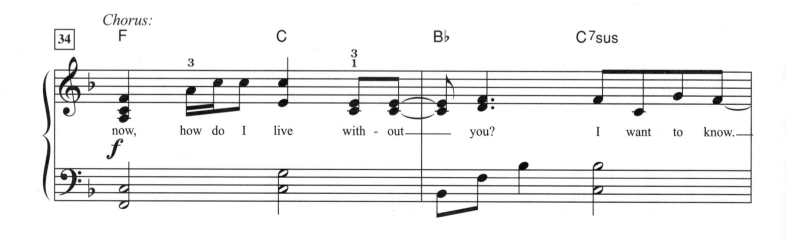

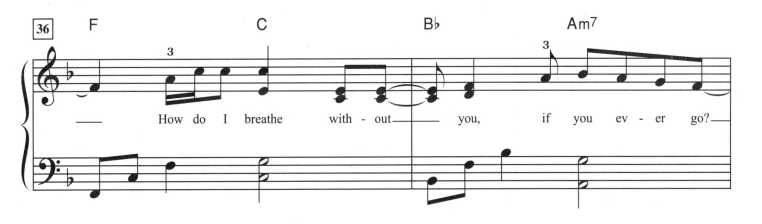

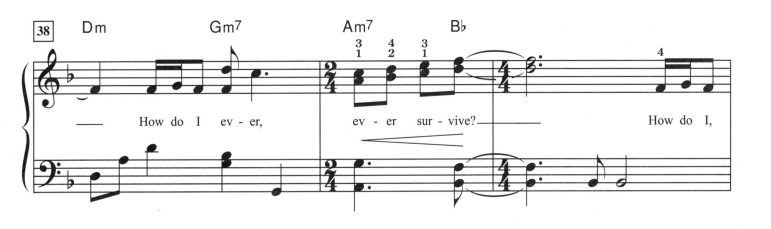

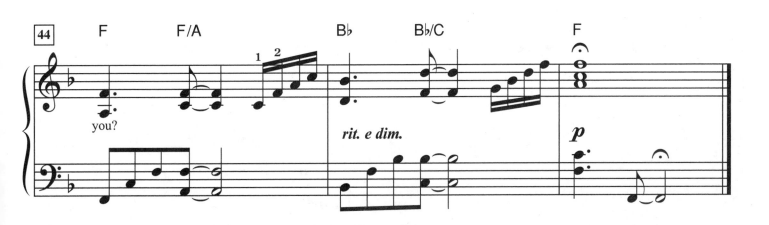

KILLING ME SOFTLY

Words and Music by
Charles Fox and Norman Gimbel
Arranged by Dan Coates

LA VIE EN ROSE

(Take Me to Your Heart Again)

Original French Lyrics By Edith Piaf
Music by Luis Guglielmi
English Lyrics by Mack David
Arranged by Dan Coates

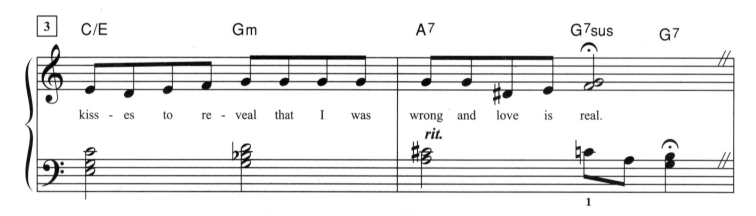

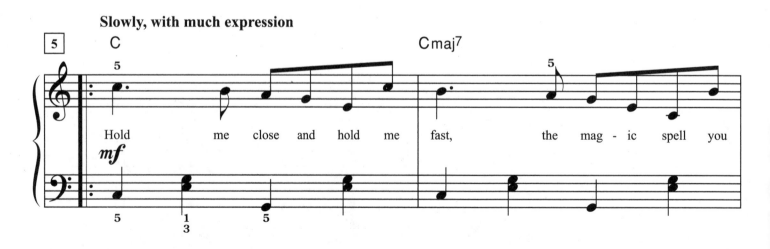

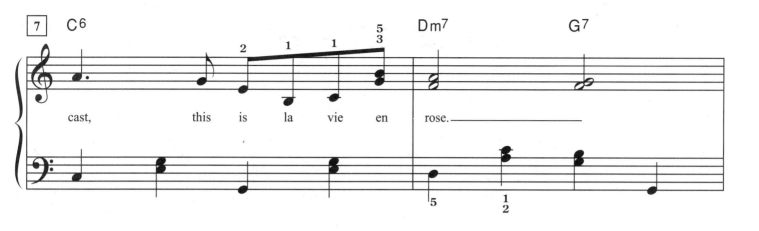

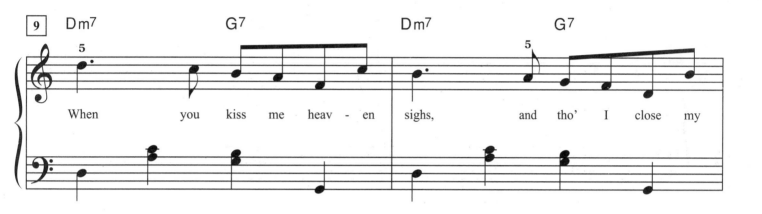

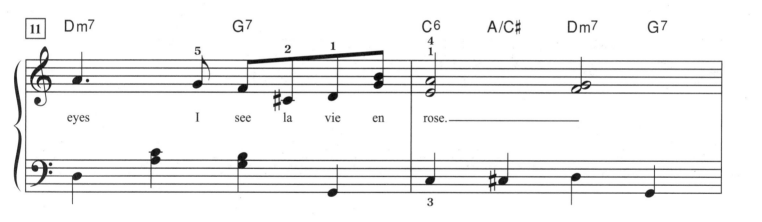

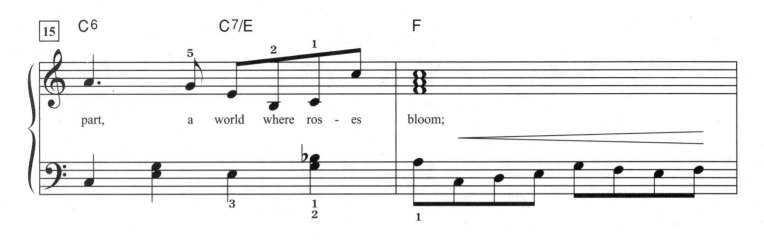

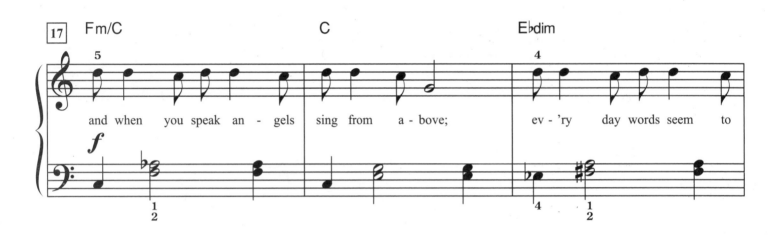

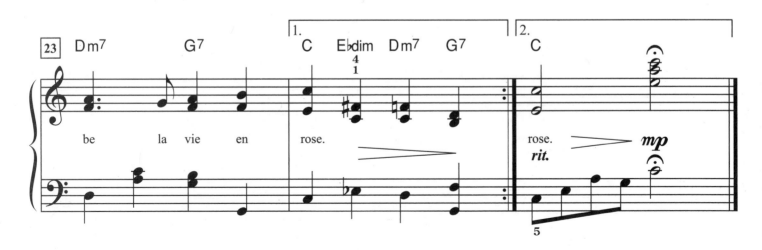

LAURA

Lyrics by Johnny Mercer
Music by David Raksin
Arranged by Dan Coates

Slowly, with expression

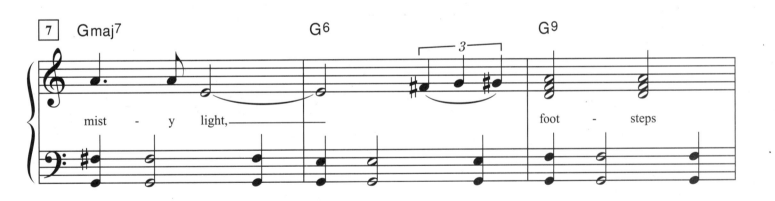

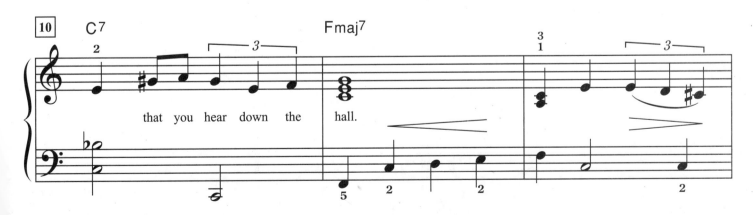

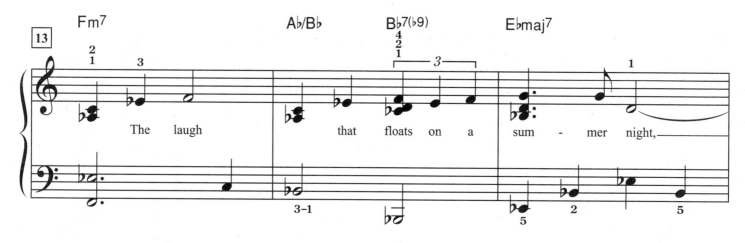

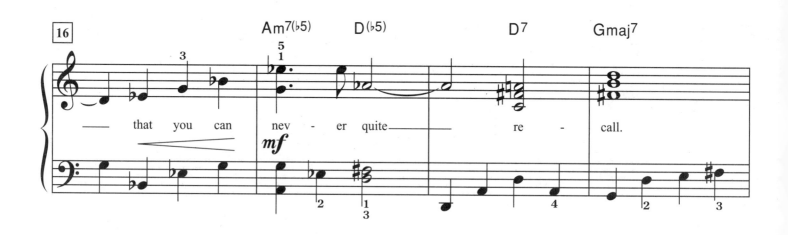

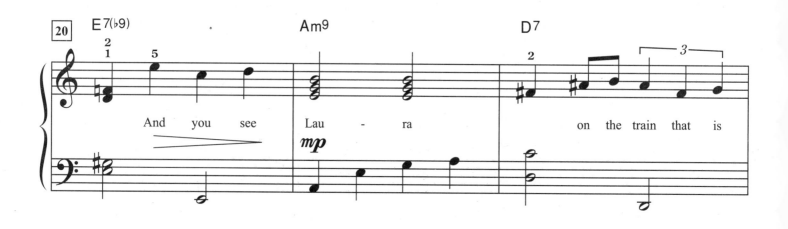

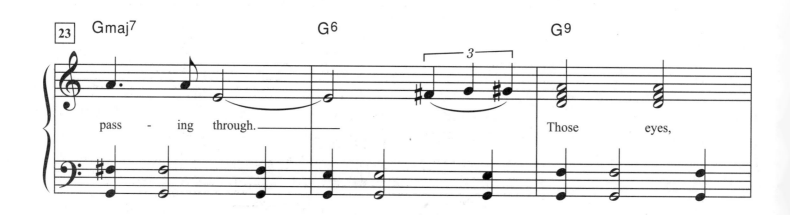

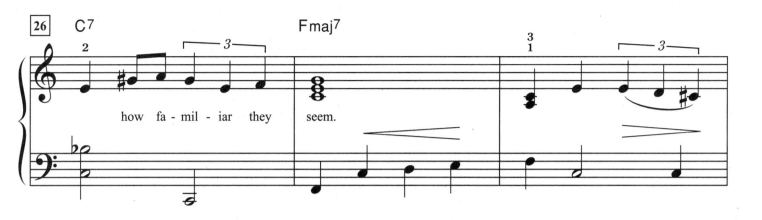

how fa - mil - iar they seem.

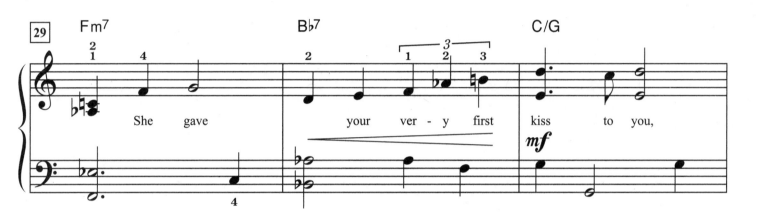

She gave your ver - y first kiss to you,

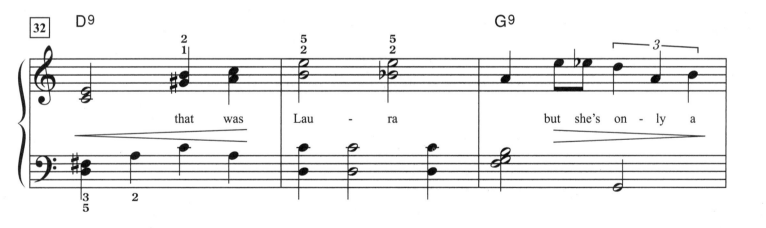

that was Lau - ra but she's on - ly a

dream. dream.

LEAVING ON A JET PLANE

Words and Music by John Denver
Arranged by Dan Coates

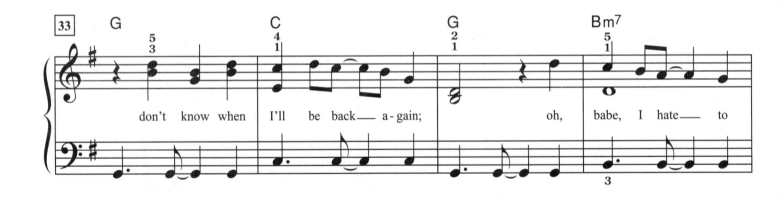

LOVE STORY

(Where Do I Begin)

Lyrics by Carl Sigman
Music by Francis Lai
Arranged by Dan Coates

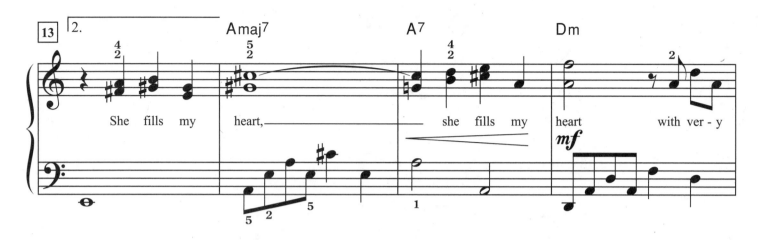

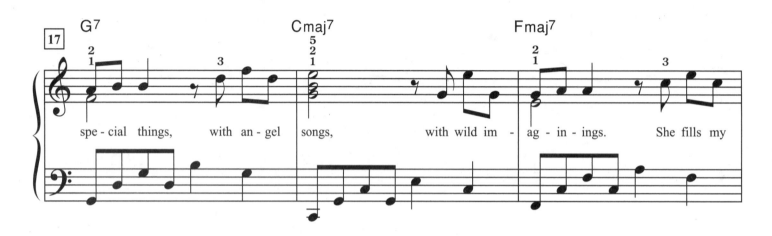

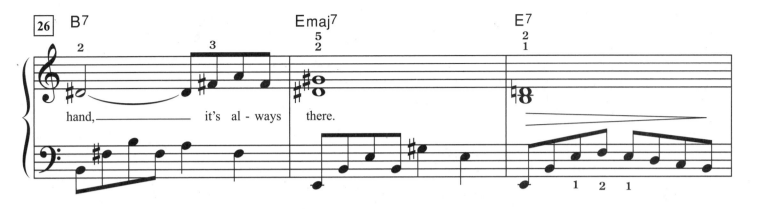

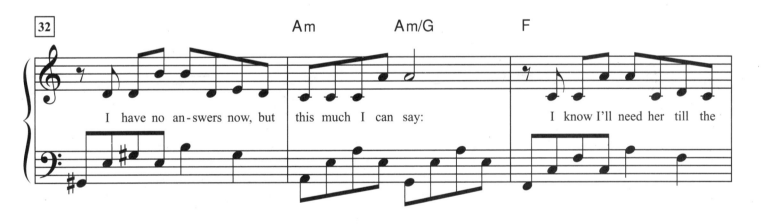

LOVE WILL LEAD YOU BACK

Words and Music by Diane Warren
Arranged by Dan Coates

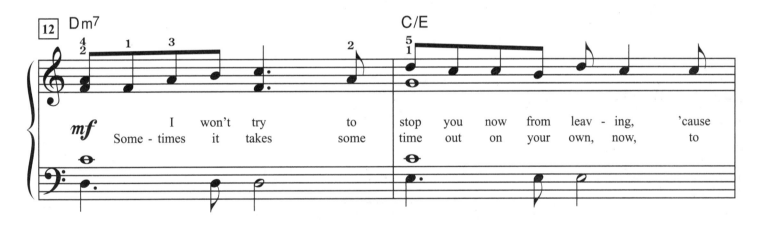

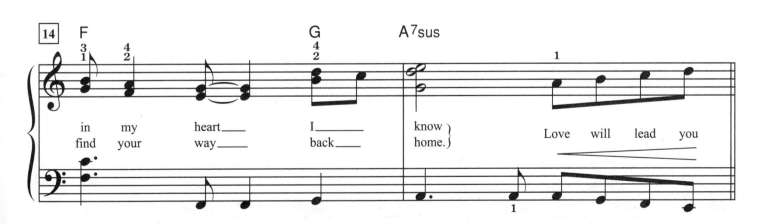

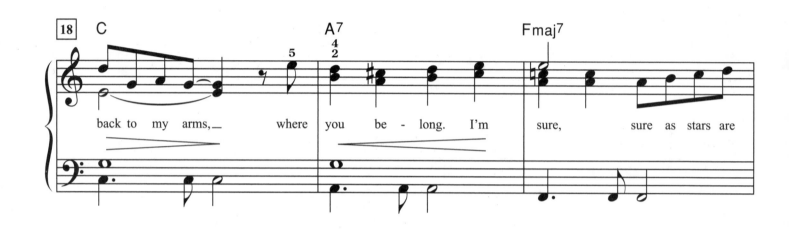

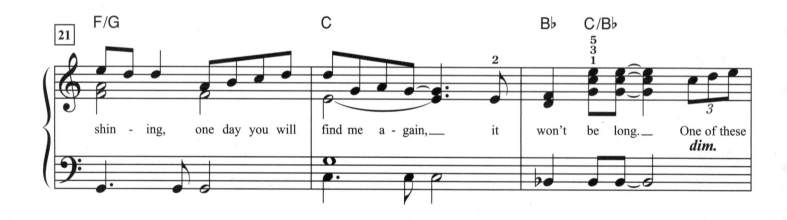

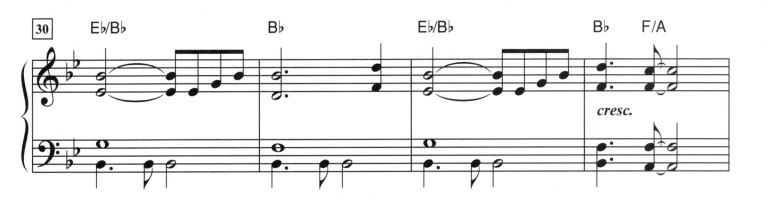

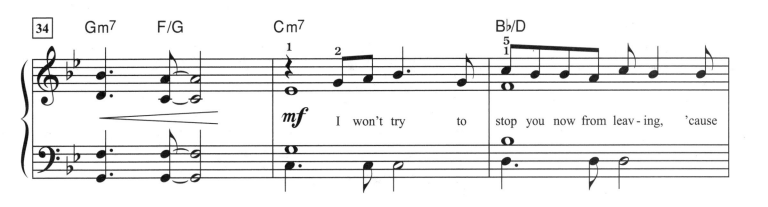

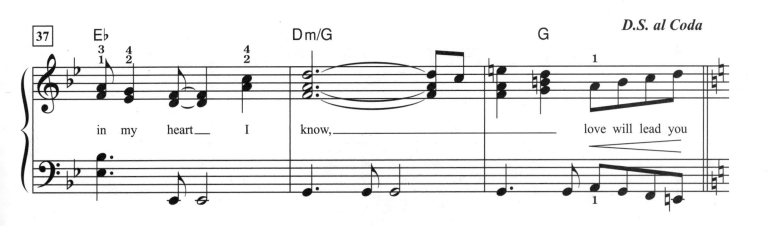

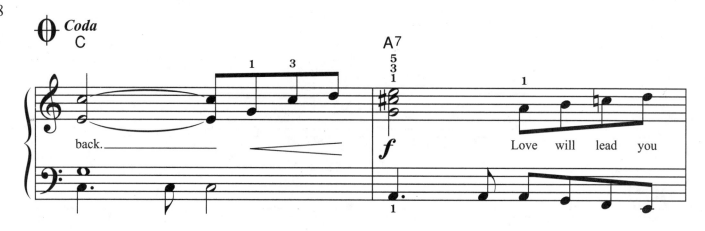

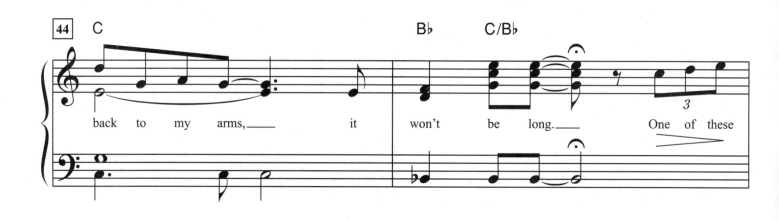

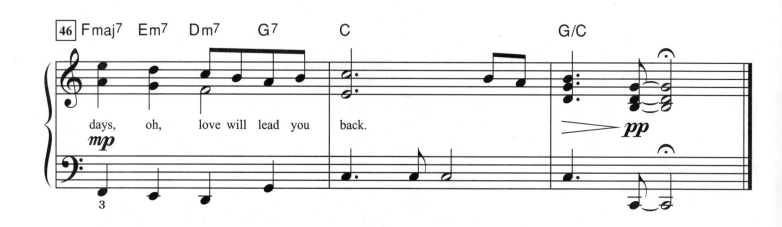

MISTY

Words by Johnny Burke
Music by Erroll Garner
Arranged by Dan Coates

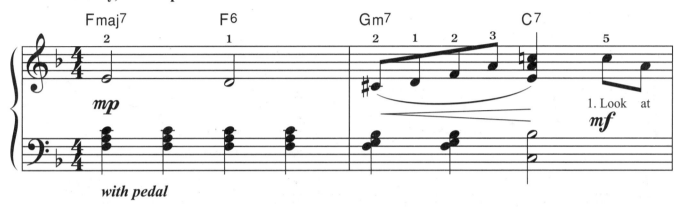

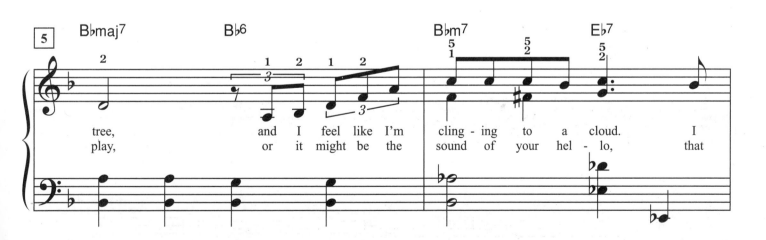

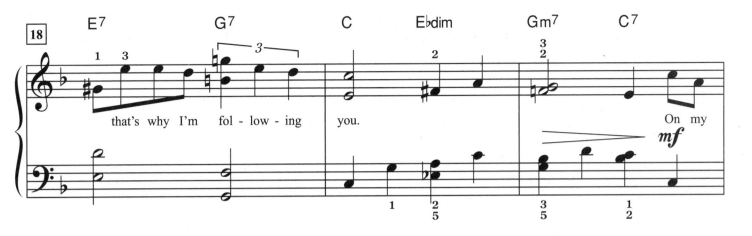

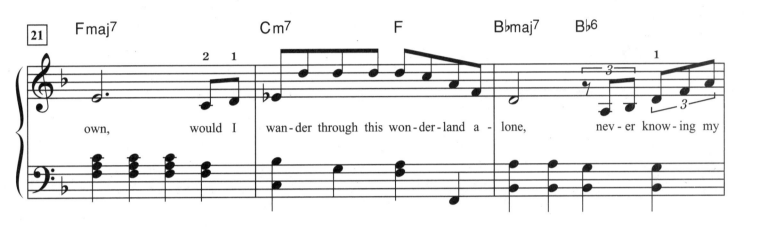

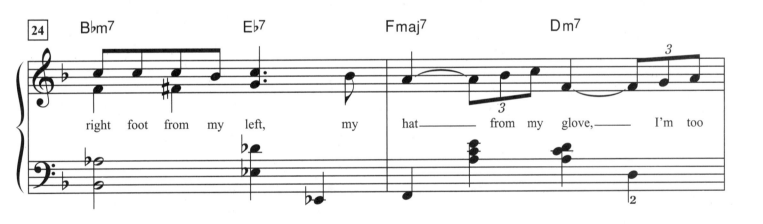

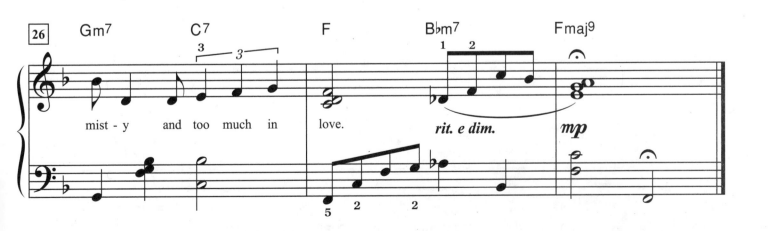

THE NOTEBOOK

(Main Title)

Written by Aaron Zigman
Arranged by Dan Coates

Slowly, with expression

ON THE STREET WHERE YOU LIVE

(from "My Fair Lady")

Words by Alan Jay Lerner
Music by Frederick Loewe
Arranged by Dan Coates

Moderately slow

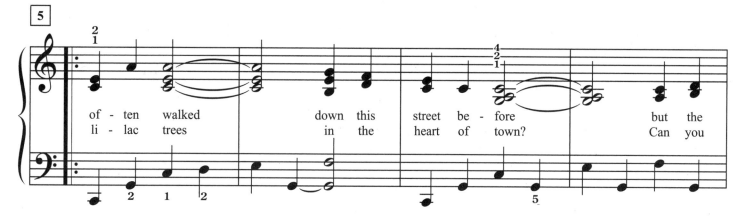

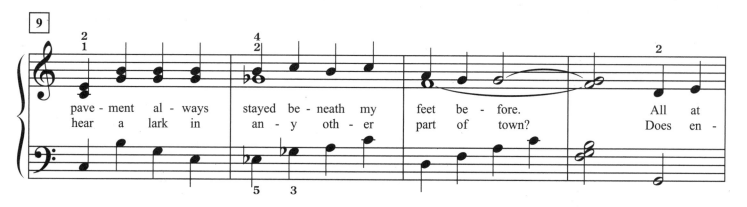

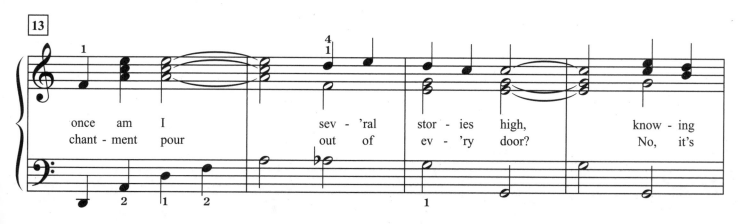

OPEN ARMS

Words and Music by
Jonathan Cain and Steve Perry
Arranged by Dan Coates

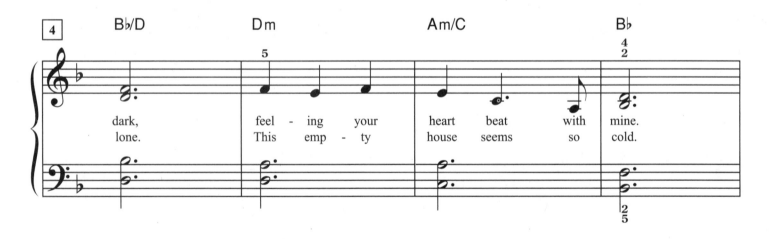

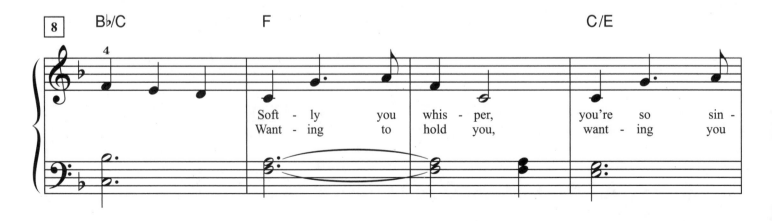

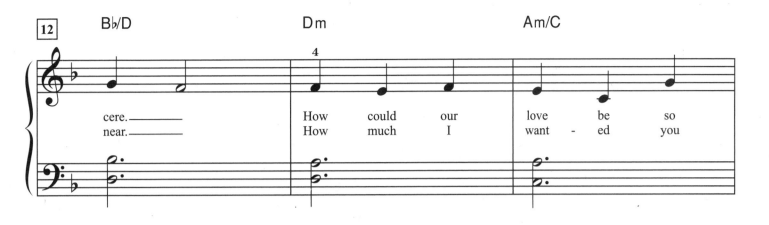

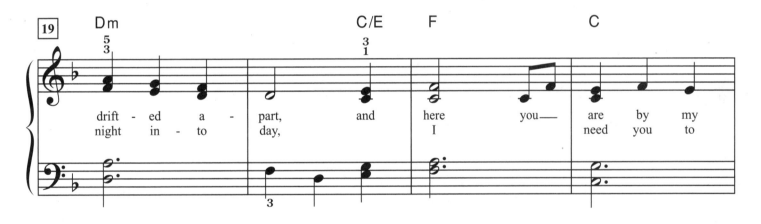

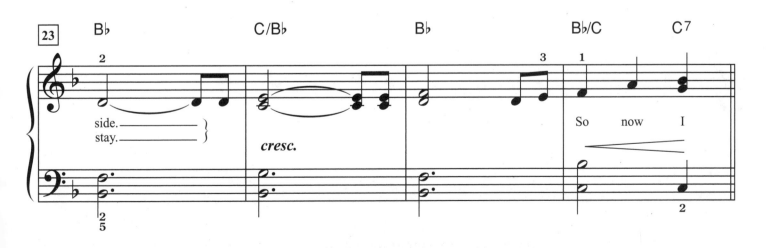

Chorus:

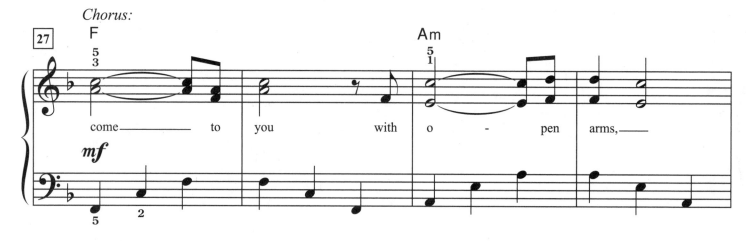

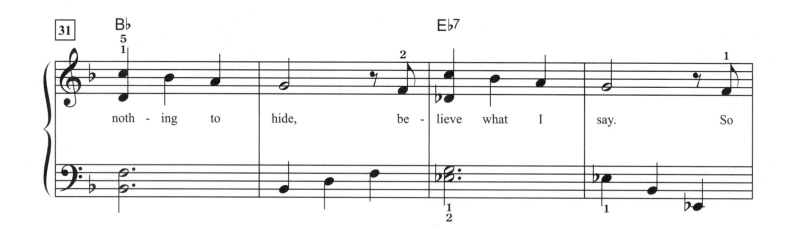

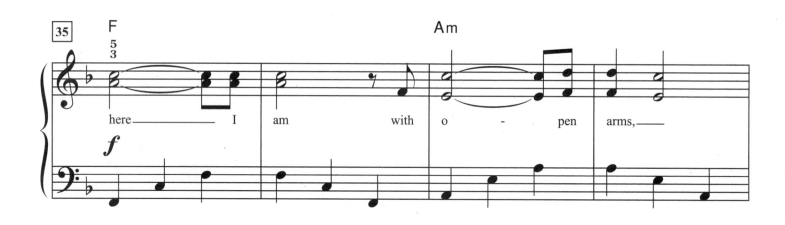

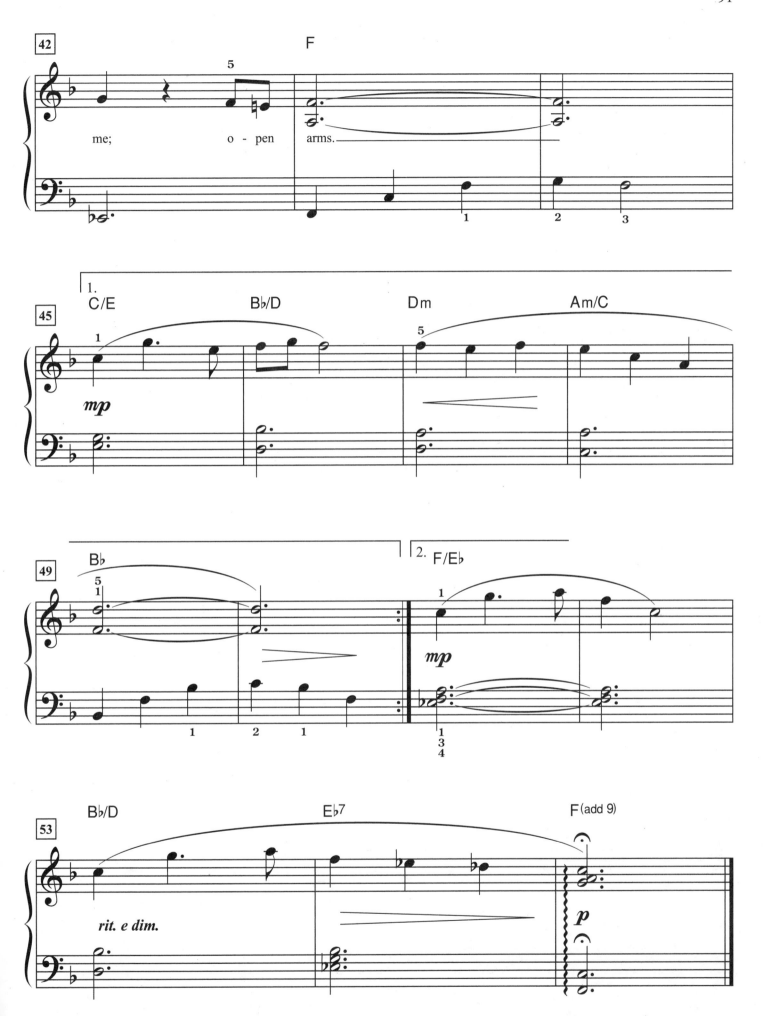

OVER THE RAINBOW

(from "The Wizard of Oz")

Music by Harold Arlen
Lyrics by E.Y. Harburg
Arranged by Dan Coates

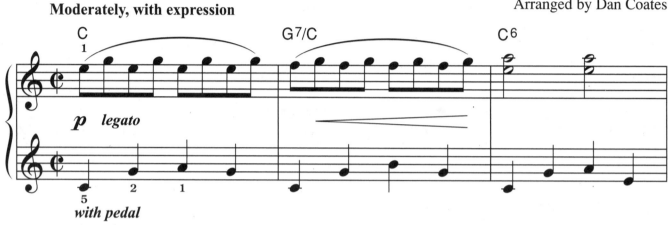

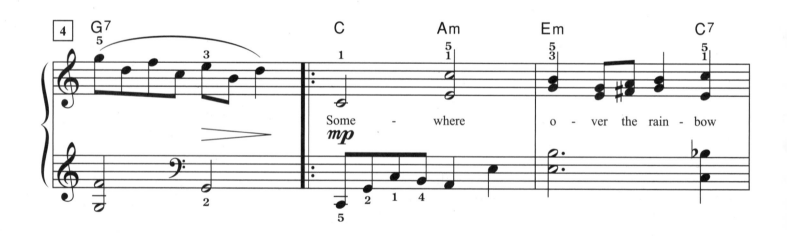

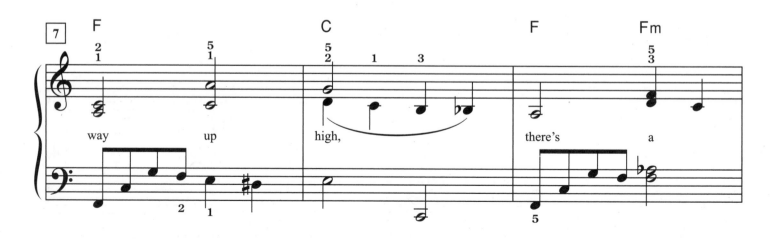

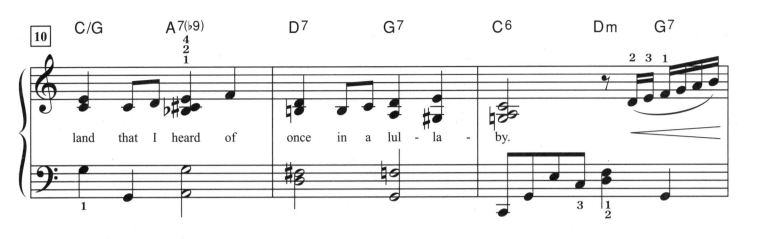

land that I heard of once in a lul - la - by.

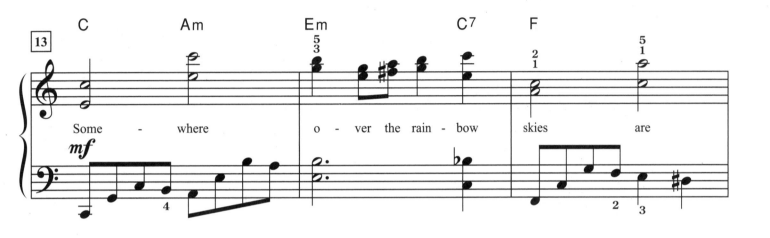

Some - where o - ver the rain - bow skies are

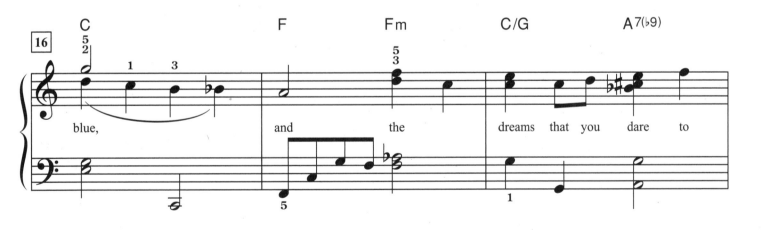

blue, and the dreams that you dare to

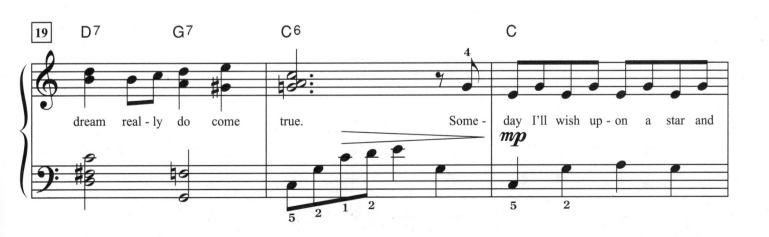

dream real - ly do come true. Some - day I'll wish up - on a star and

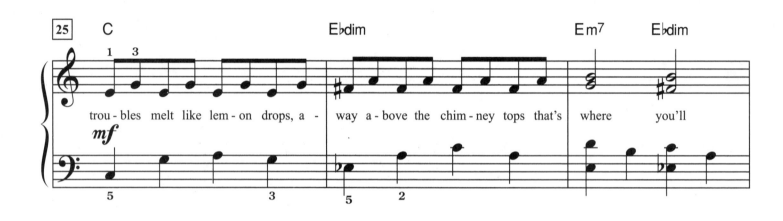

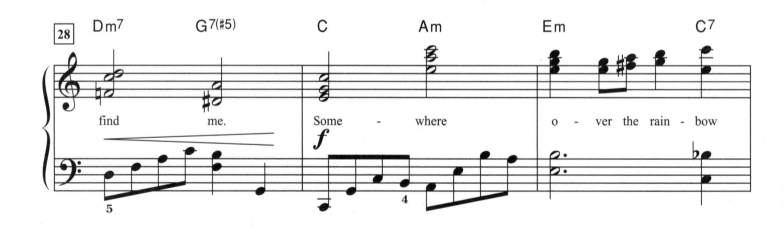

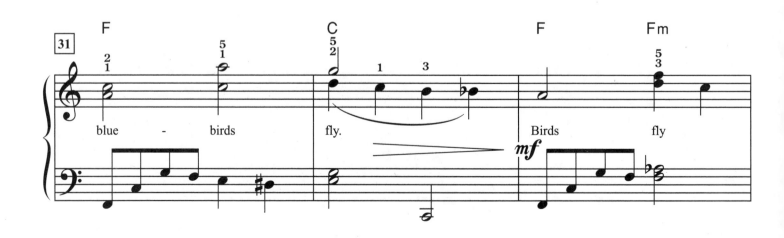

PEOPLE

(from "Funny Girl")

Words by Bob Merrill
Music by Jule Styne
Arranged by Dan Coates

Steady, with feeling

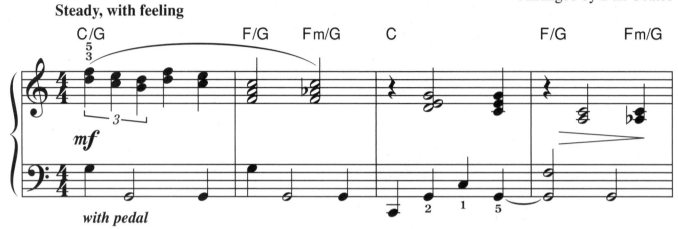

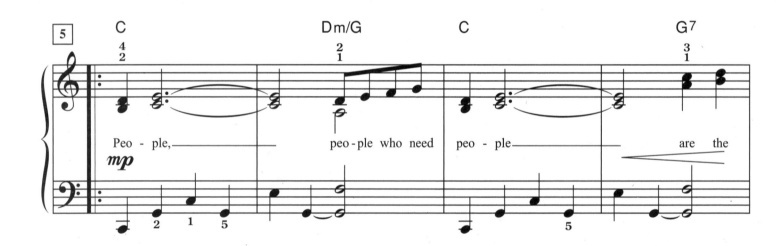

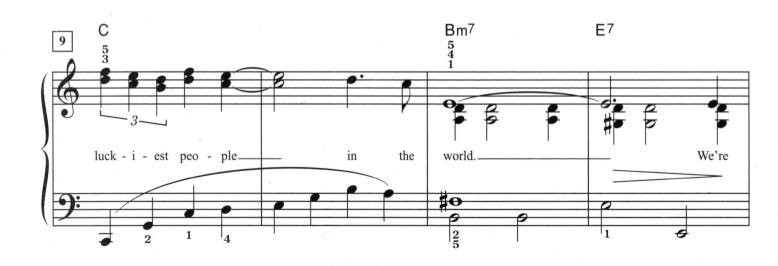

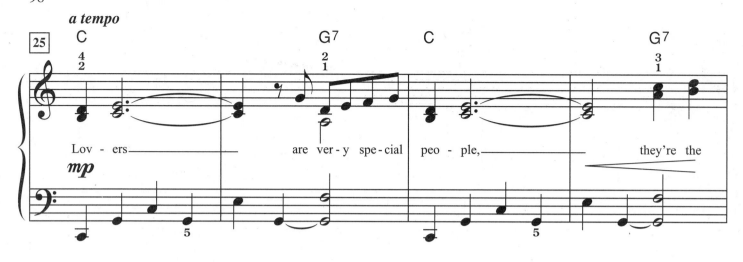

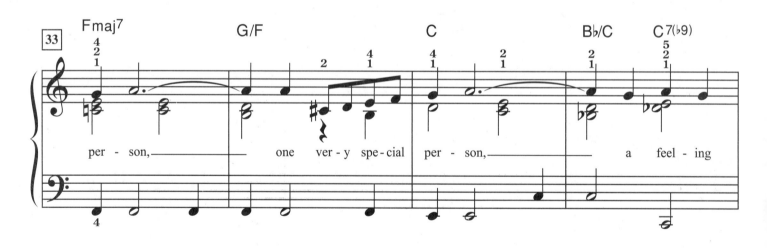

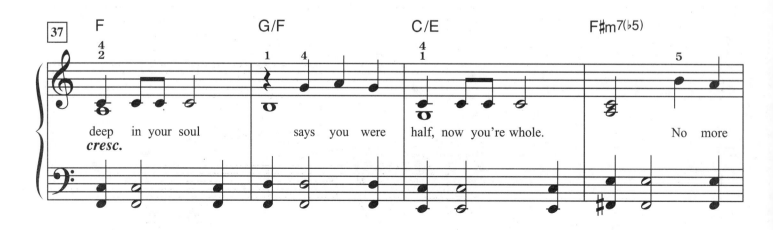

THE PRAYER

Words and Music by
Carole Bayer Sager and David Foster
Arranged by Dan Coates

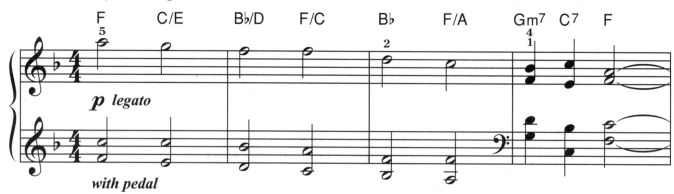

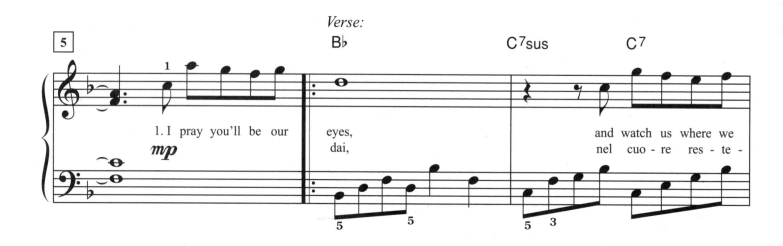

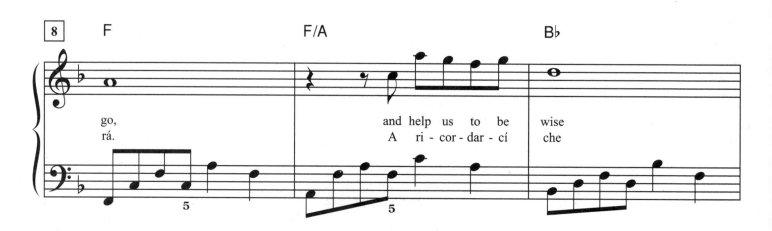

Bridge:

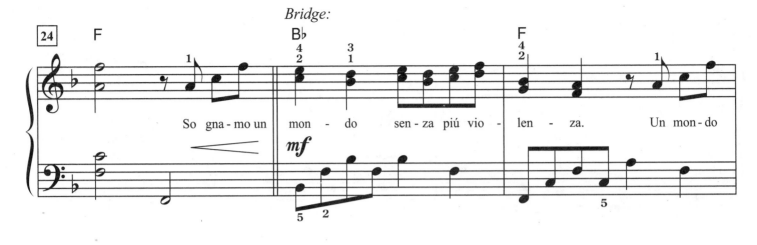

So gna - mo un mon - do sen - za piú vio - len - za. Un mon - do

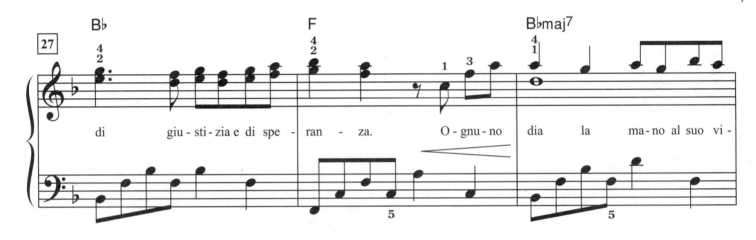

di giu - sti - zia e di spe - ran - za. O - gnu - no dia la ma - no al suo vi -

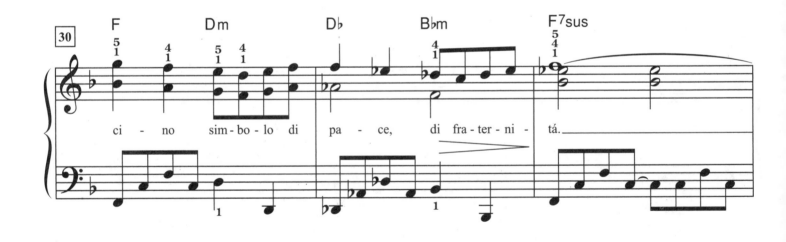

ci - no sim - bo - lo di pa - ce, di fra - ter - ni - tá. ____

Verse:

____ 3. We ask that life be kind, and watch us from a -

bove.　　　　　　We hope each soul will　find

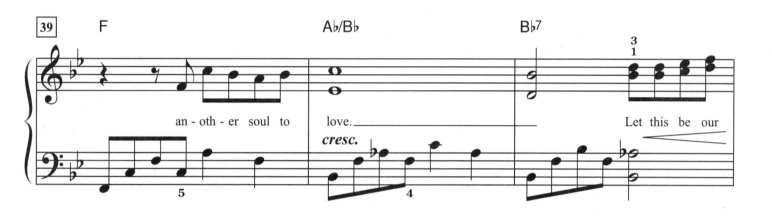

an - oth - er soul to　love.　　　　　Let this be our

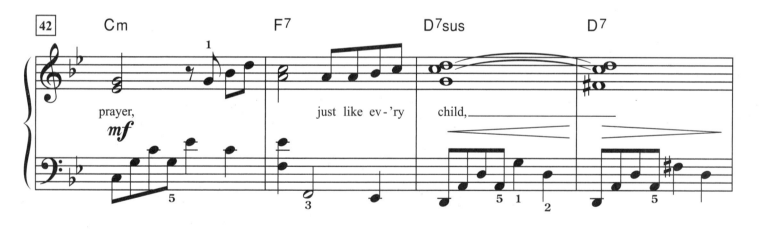

prayer,　　　　just like ev - 'ry　child,

need to find a place,　　guide us with your grace.　　Give us faith so we'll　be

safe. E la fe-de che hai a-cce-so in noi.

Sen-to che ci sal-ve- rá. *rit. e dim.*

Verse 2 (English lyric):
I pray we'll find your light,
And hold it in our hearts
When stars go out each night.
Let this be our prayer,
When shadows fill our day.
Lead us to a place,
Guide us with your grace.
Give us faith so we'll be safe.

Verse 3 (Italian lyric):
La forza che ci dai
é il desiderio che.
Ognuno trovi amore
Intorno e dentro sé.

THE PROMISE

Composed by Jim Brickman
Arranged by Dan Coates

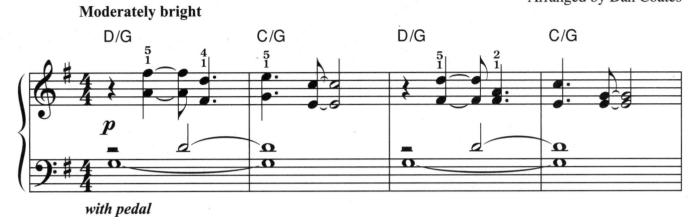

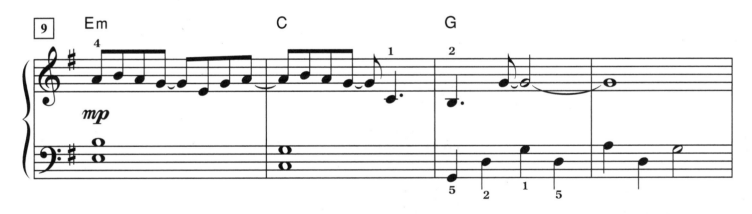

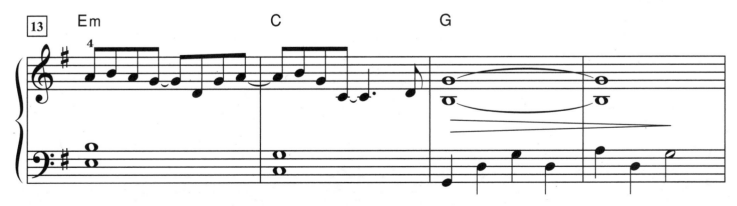

RIGHT HERE WAITING

Words and Music by Richard Marx
Arranged by Dan Coates

Moderately, with expression

Verse:

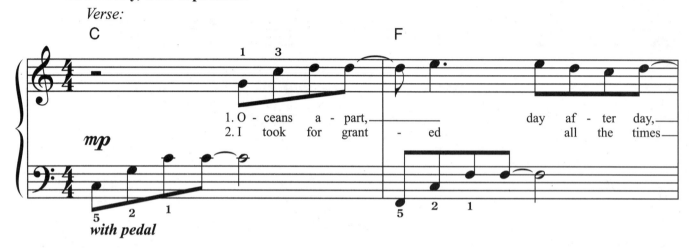

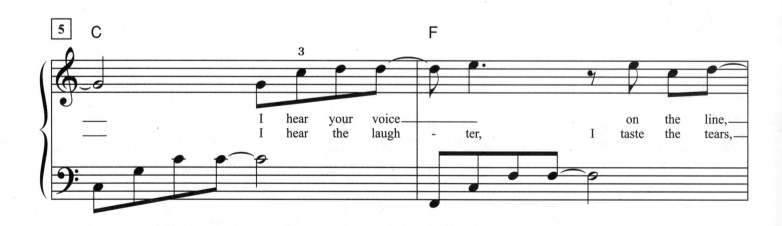

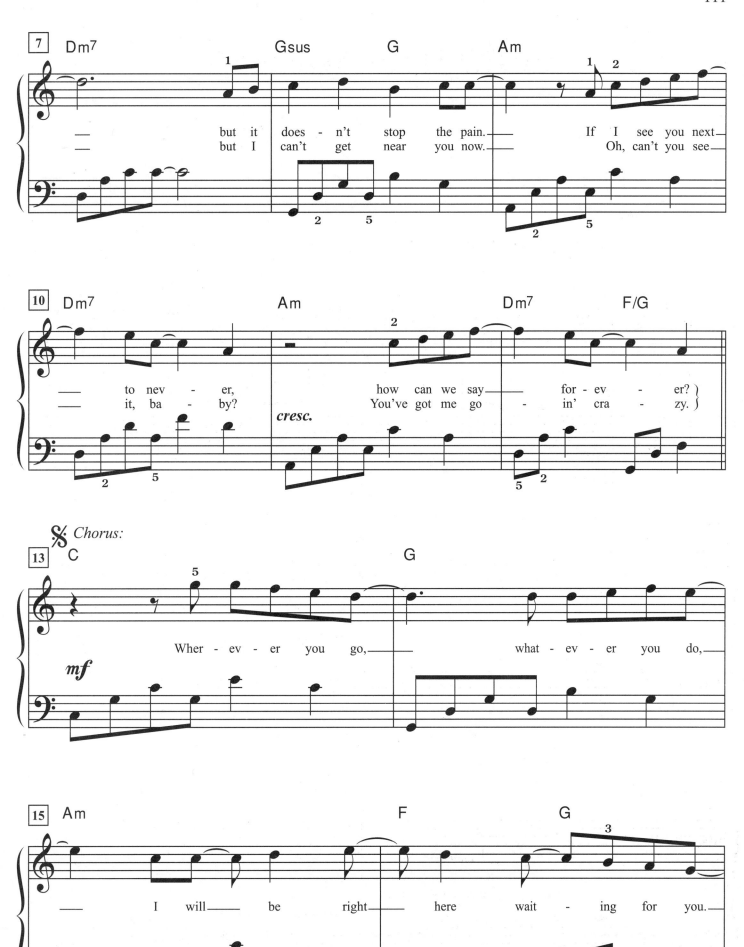

What - ev - er it takes, or how my heart breaks,

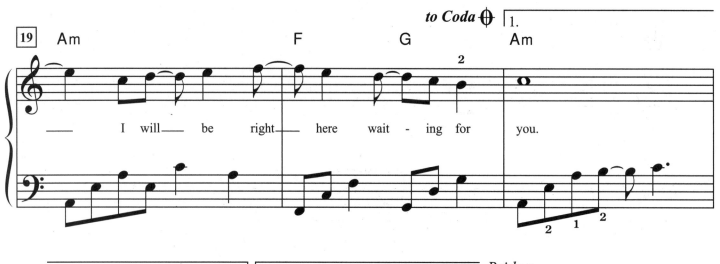

to Coda ⊕ | 1.

I will be right here wait - ing for you.

| 2.   *Bridge:*

you. I won - der how we can sur - vive

this ro - mance. But in the

SHADOW OF YOUR SMILE

(from "The Sandpiper")

Lyric by Paul Francis Webster
Music by Johnny Mandel
Arranged by Dan Coates

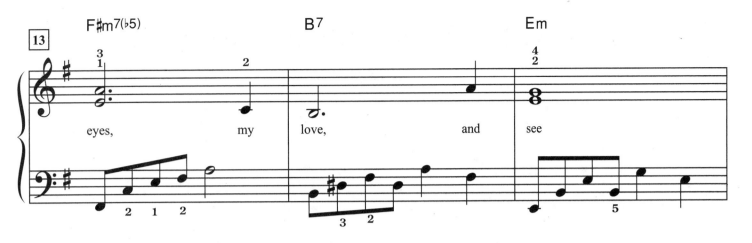
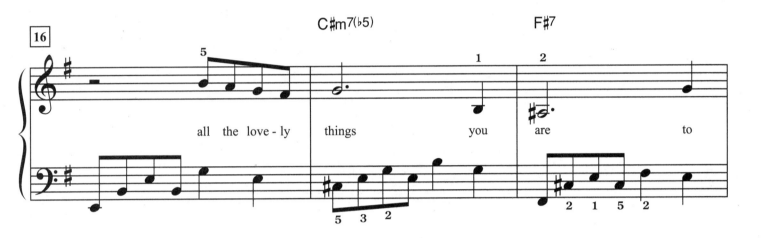

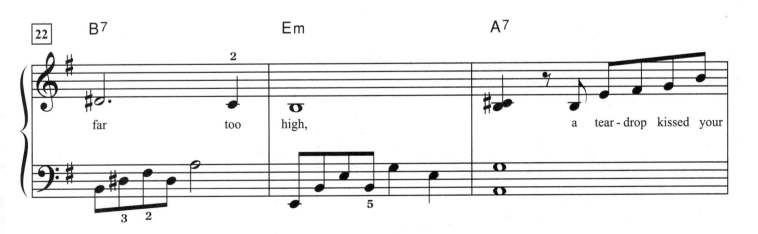

UN-BREAK MY HEART

(Regresa a Mi)

Words and Music by Diane Warren
Arranged by Dan Coates

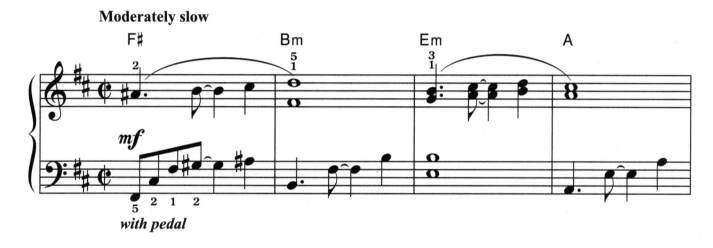

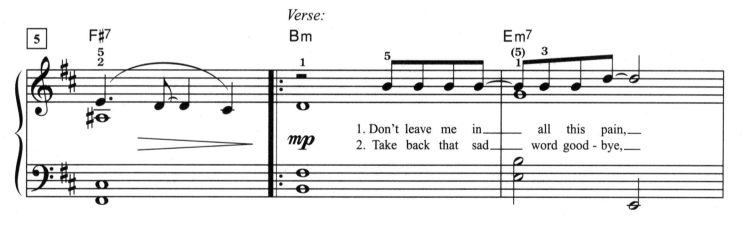

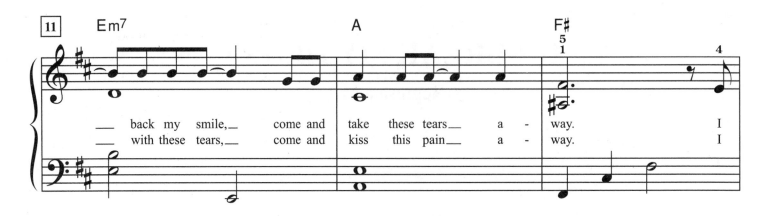

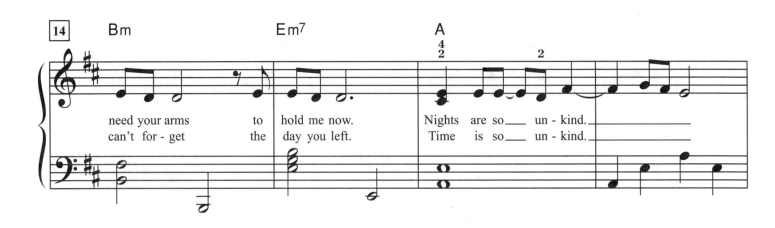

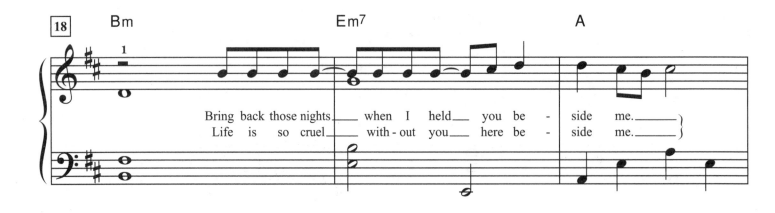

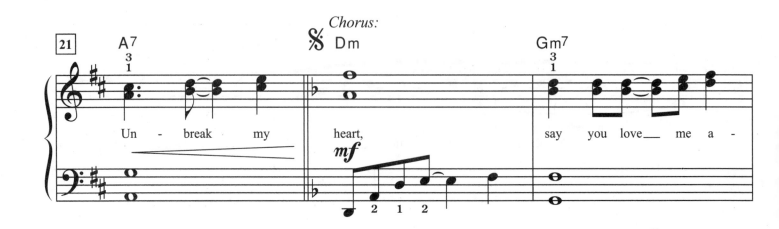

gain. Un - do___ this hurt you caused___ when you

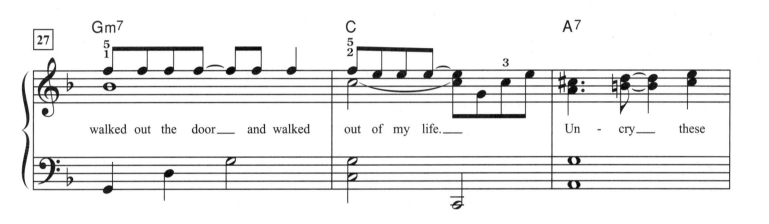

walked out the door___ and walked out of my life.___ Un - cry___ these

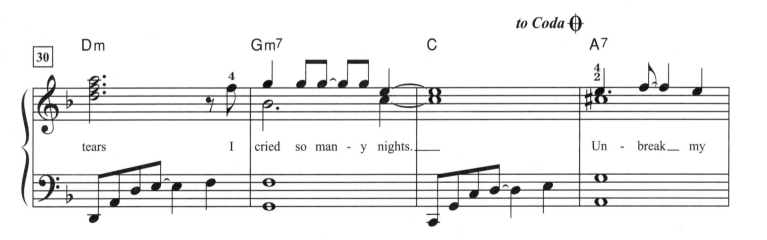

to Coda

tears I cried so man - y nights.___ Un - break___ my

heart.___

dim.

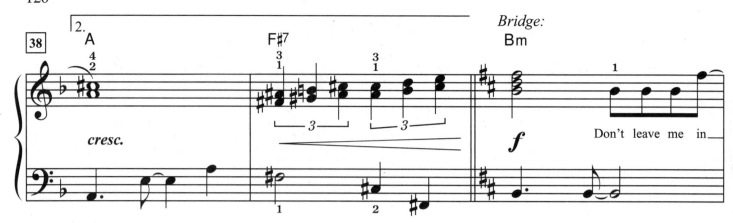

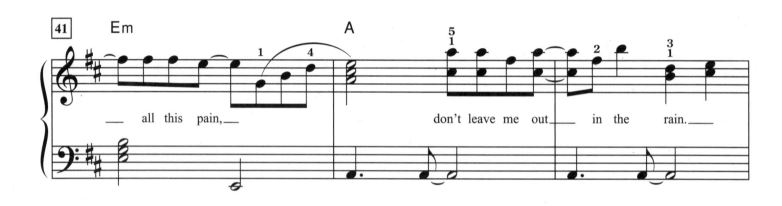

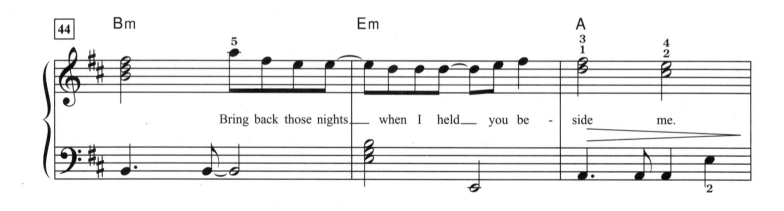

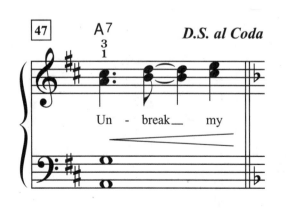
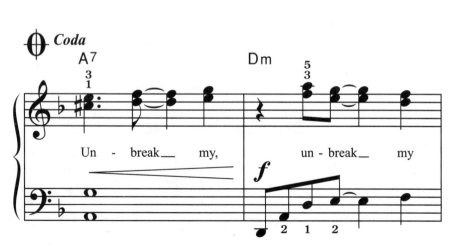

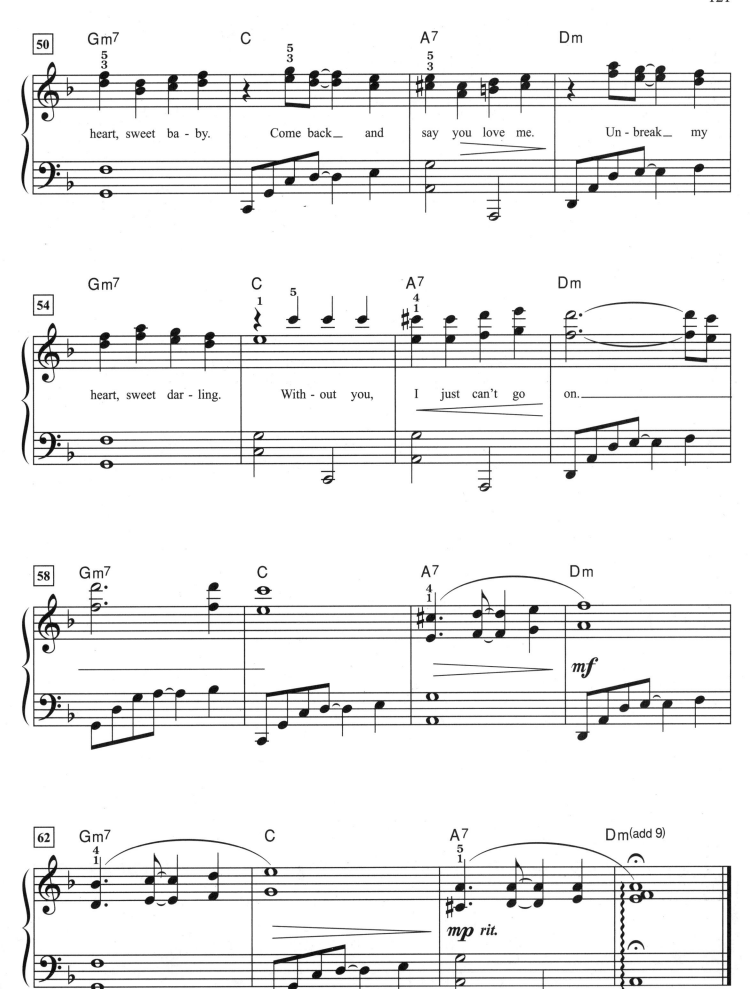

SUMMERTIME

(from "Porgy and Bess")

Music and Lyrics by George Gershwin,
DuBose and Dorothy Heyward and Ira Gershwin
Arranged by Dan Coates

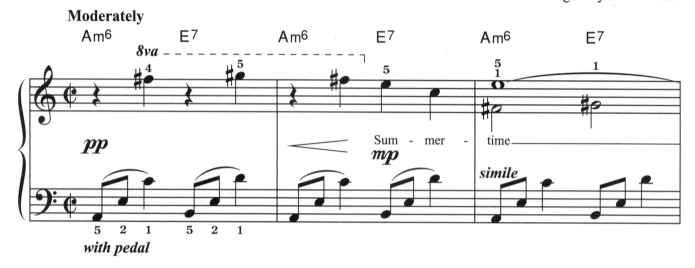

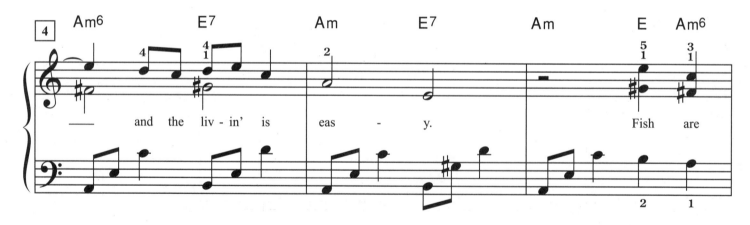

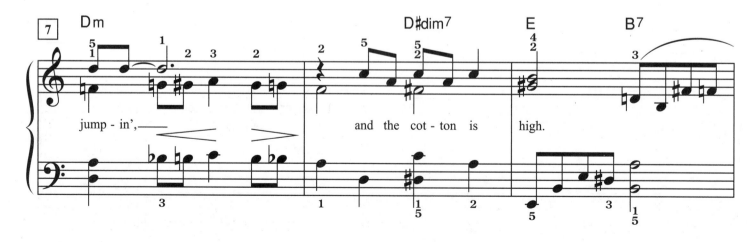

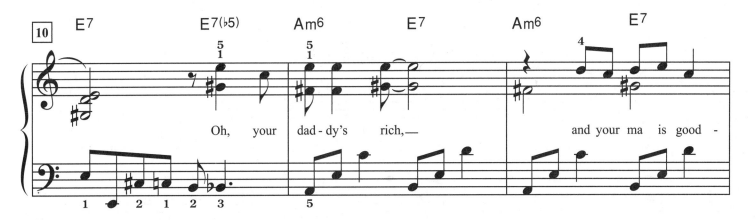

Oh, your dad-dy's rich,— and your ma is good-

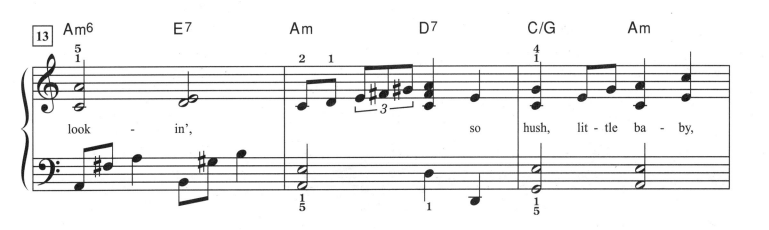

look - in', so hush, lit - tle ba - by,

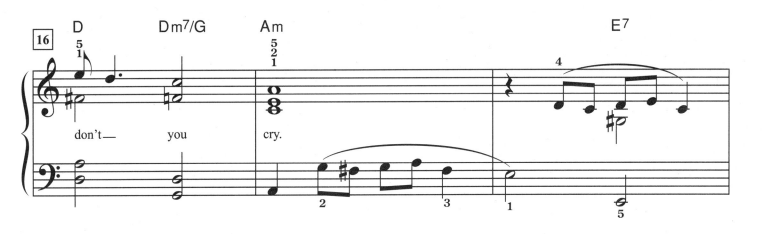

don't— you cry.

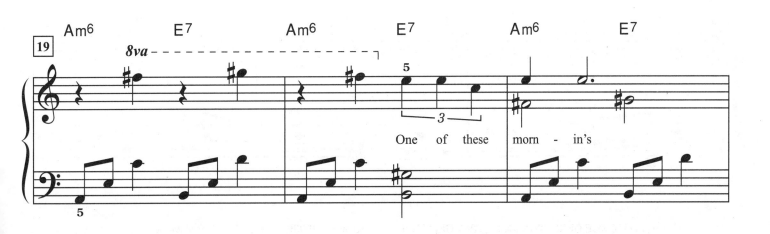

One of these morn - in's

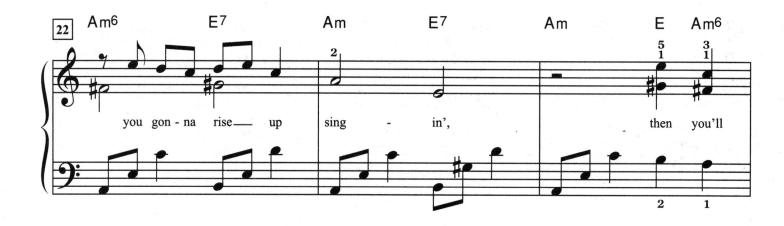

22 | Am6 — E7 — Am — E7 — Am — E — Am6

you gon-na rise—— up sing - in', then you'll

25 | Dm — D♯dim — E — B7

spread your wings and you'll take to the sky.

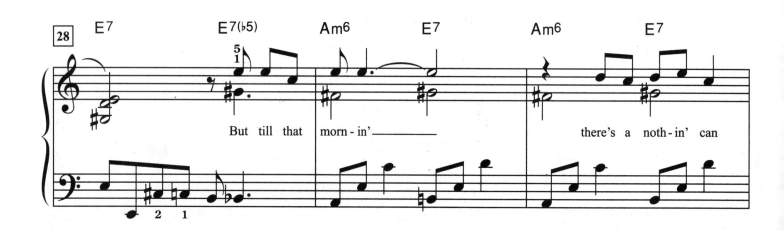

28 | E7 — E7(♭5) — Am6 — E7 — Am6 — E7

But till that morn-in'———— there's a noth-in' can

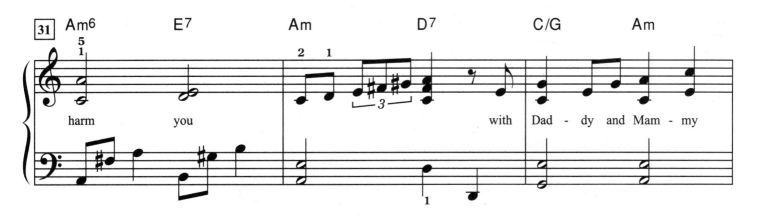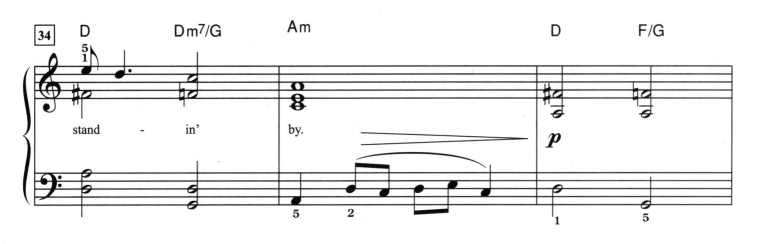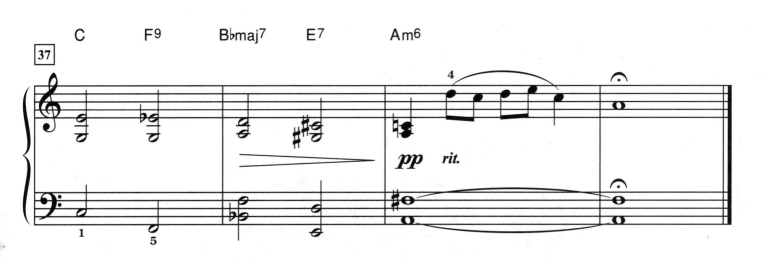

TAKE MY BREATH AWAY

Music by Giorgio Moroder
Words by Tom Whitlock
Arranged by Dan Coates

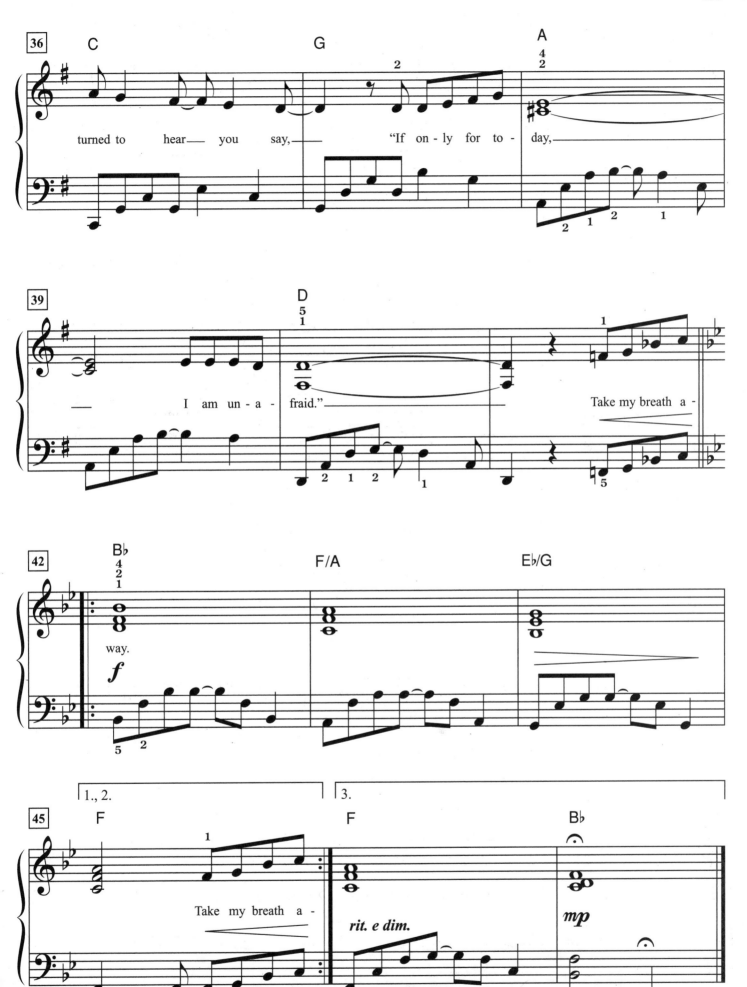

VALENTINE

Words and Music by
Jim Brickman and Jack Kugell
Arranged by Dan Coates

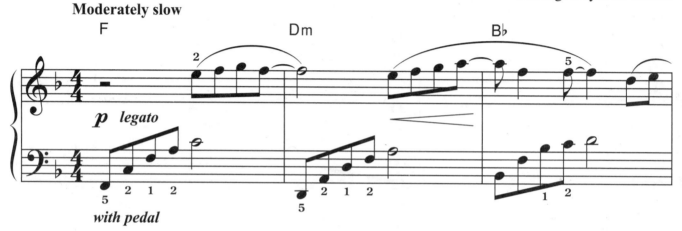

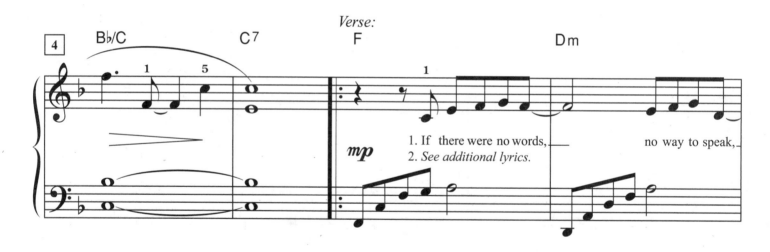

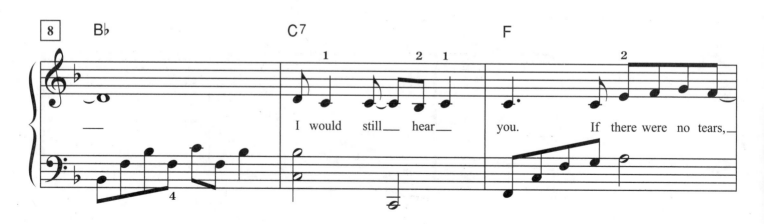

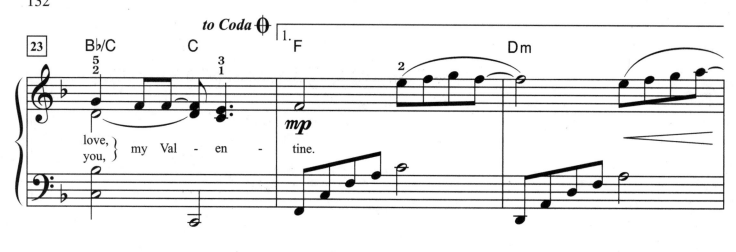

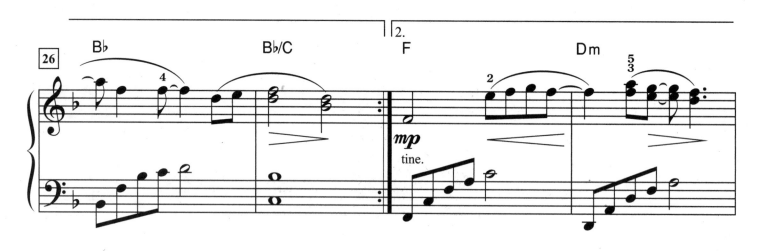

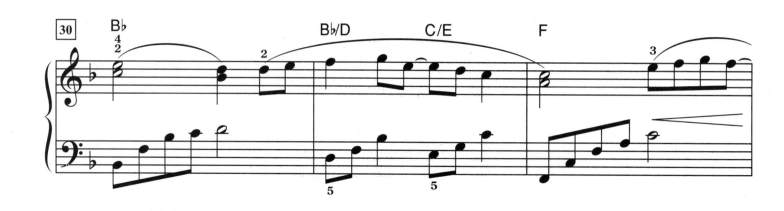

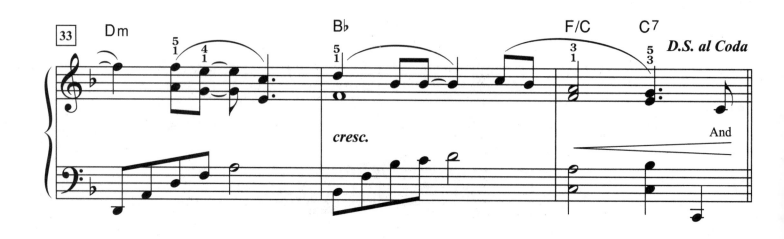

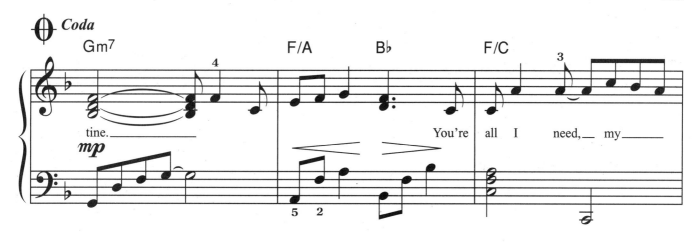

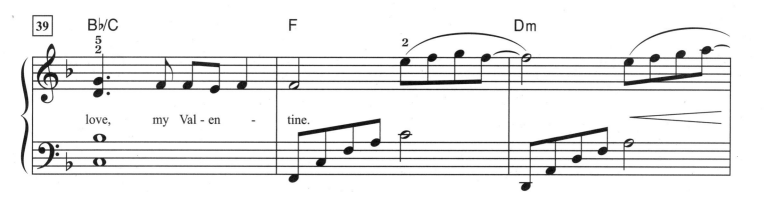

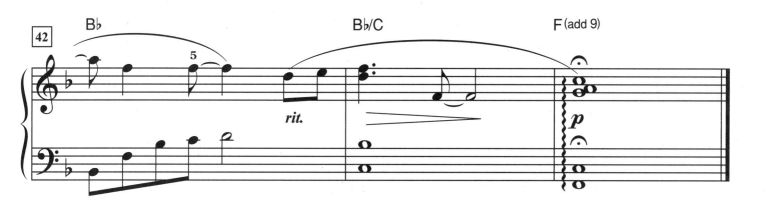

Verse 2:
All of my life,
I have been waiting for all you give to me.
You've opened my eyes
And shown me how to love unselfishly.
I've dreamed of this a thousand times before,
But in my dreams I couldn't love you more.
I will give you my heart until the end of time.
You're all I need, my love,
My Valentine.

WIND BENEATH MY WINGS

(from "Beaches")

Words and Music by
Larry Henley and Jeff Silbar
Arranged by Dan Coates

Slowly

Verse:

1. It must have been cold____ there____ in my
2. I was the one____ with____ all the

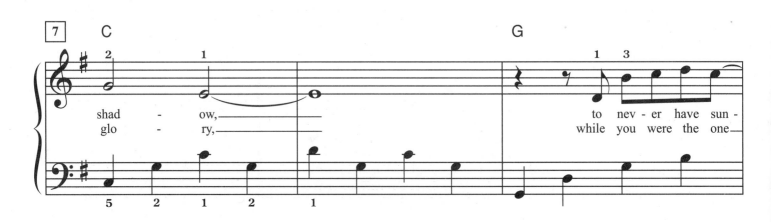

shad - ow,____
glo - ry,____

to nev - er have sun
while you were the one

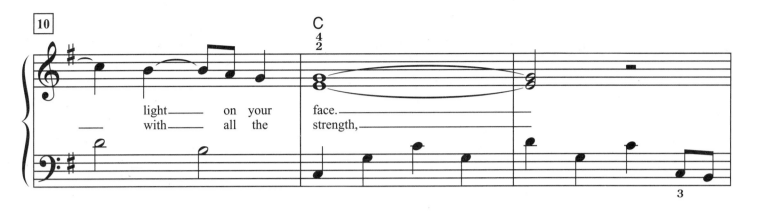

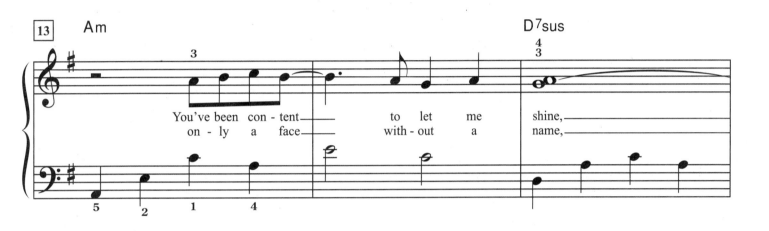

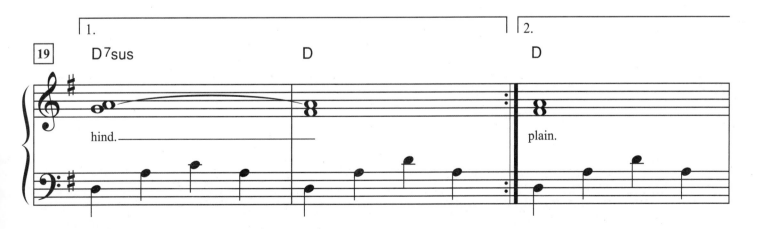

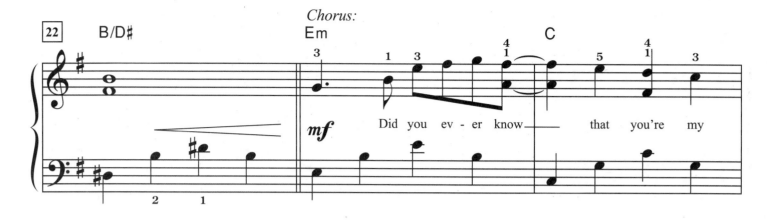

Chorus:

Did you ev - er know____ that you're my

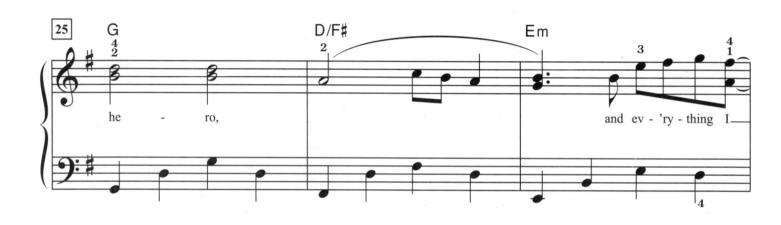

he - ro,____ and ev - 'ry - thing I____

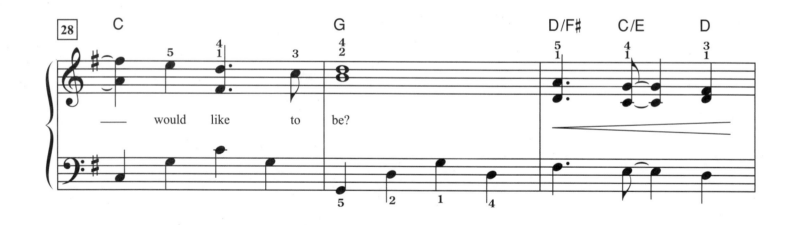

____ would like to be?

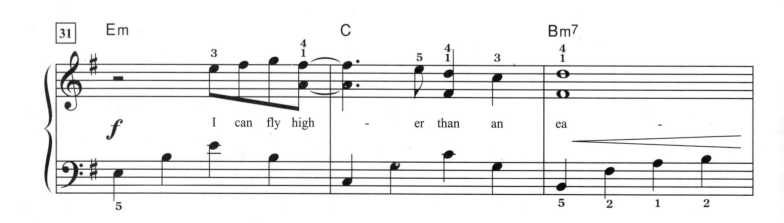

I can fly high - er than an ea -

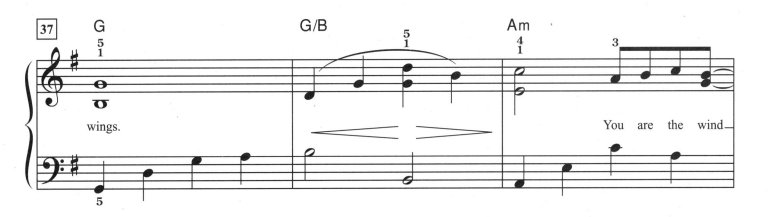

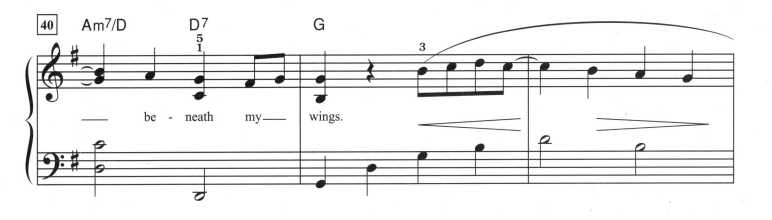

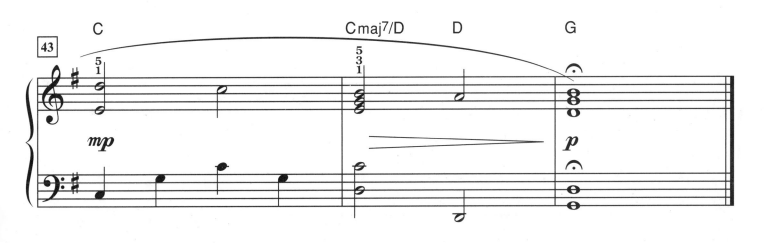

YOU LIGHT UP MY LIFE

Words and Music by Joe Brooks
Arranged by Dan Coates

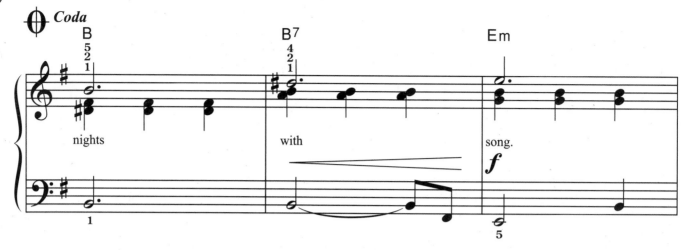

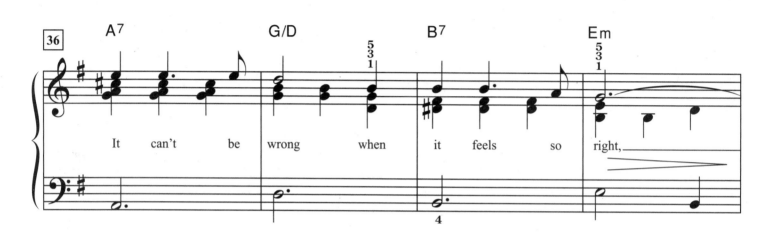

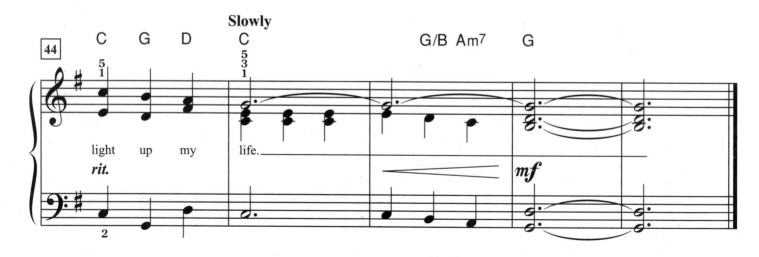

YOU NEEDED ME

Words and Music by Randy Goodrum
Arranged by Dan Coates

YOU RAISE ME UP

Words and Music by
Rolf Lovland and Brendan Graham
Arranged by Dan Coates

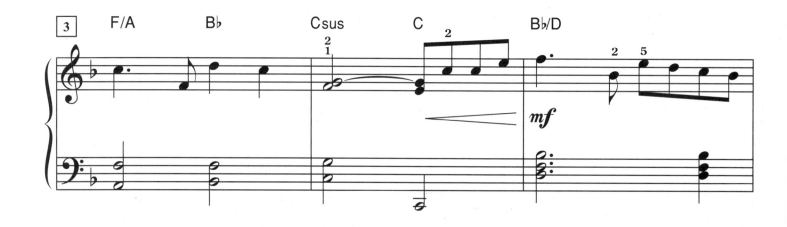

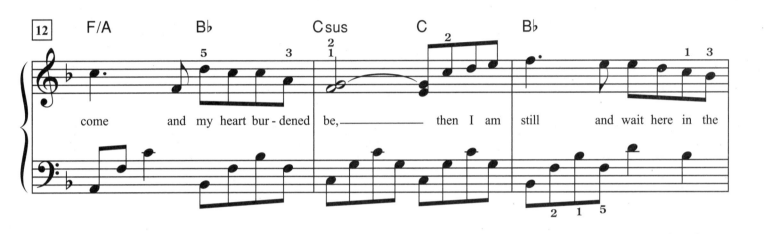

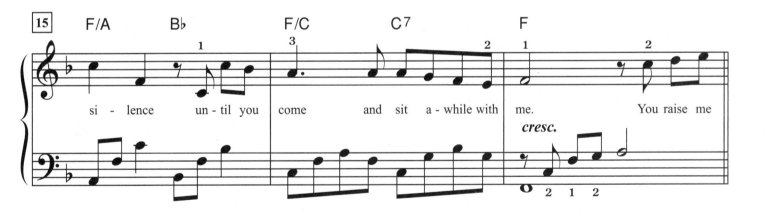

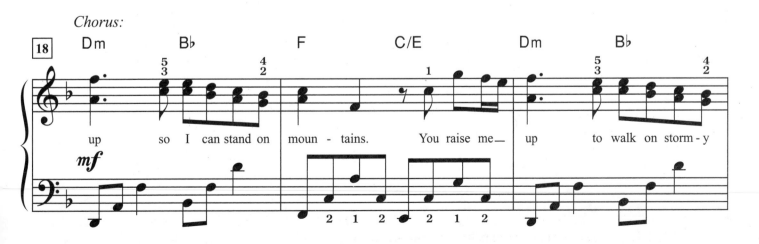

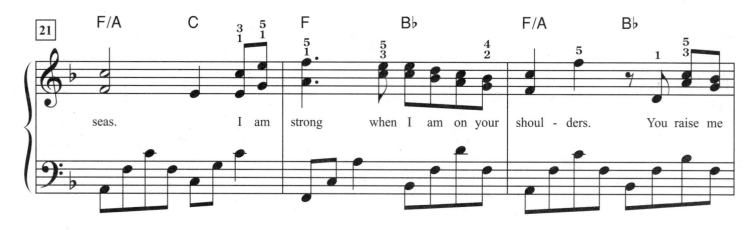

seas.   I am   strong   when I am on your   shoul - ders.   You raise me

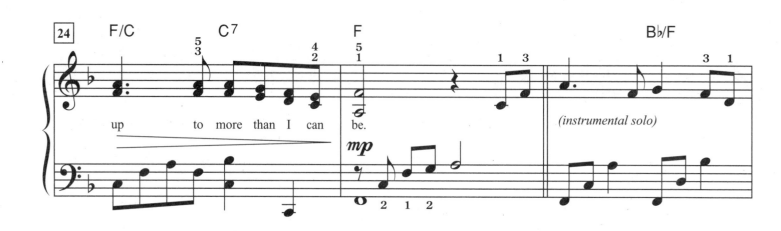

up   to more than I can   be.   *(instrumental solo)*

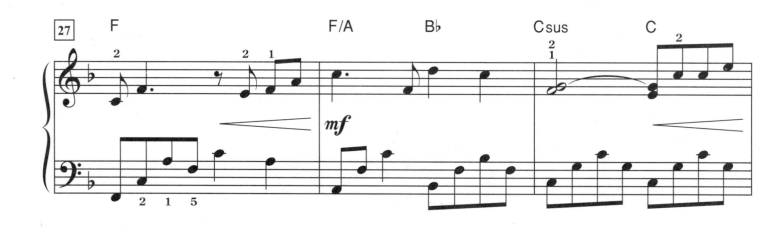

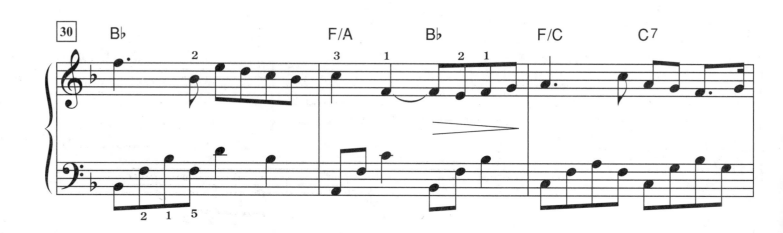

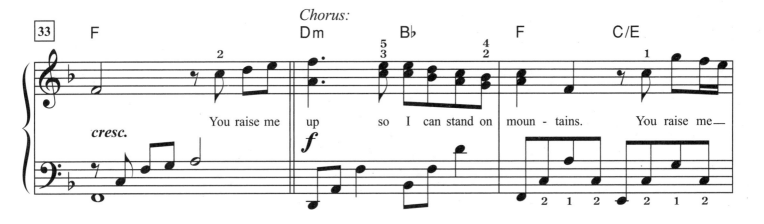

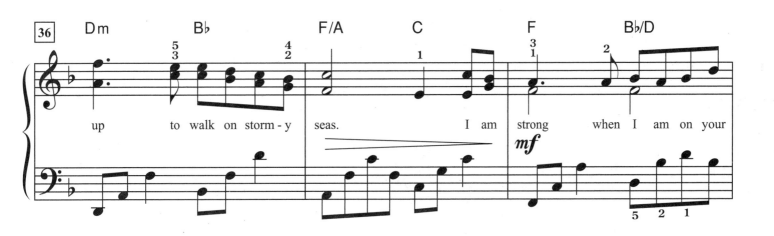

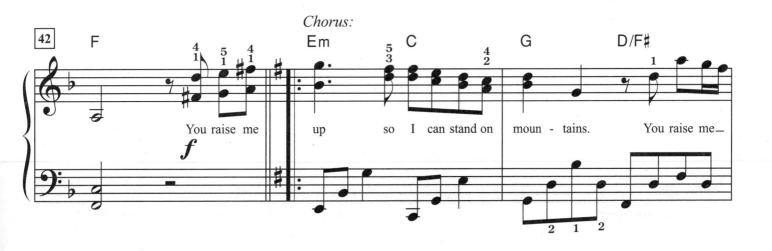

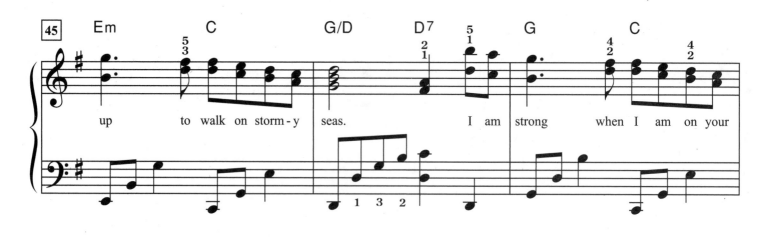

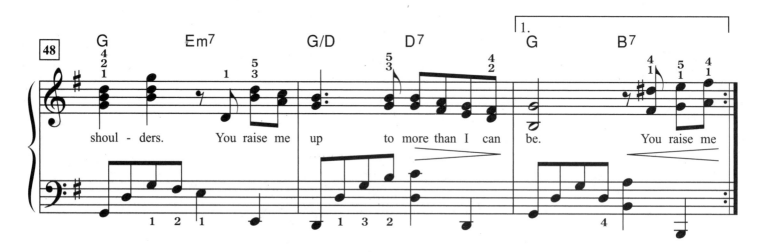

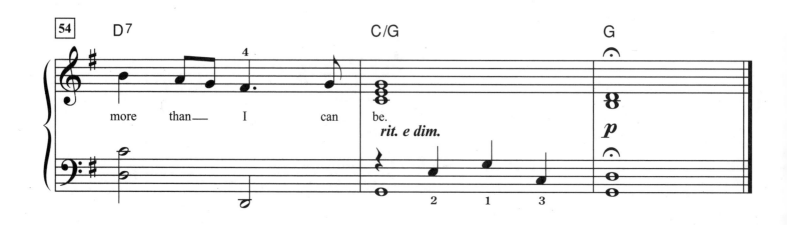